The Polish

Seventeenth Edition

Georgia Perimeter College

Editors

Na Keya H. Bazemore

Kenneth McNamara   Michael Hall

Cover image © Shutterstock, Inc.

www.kendallhunt.com
Send all inquiries to:
4050 Westmark Drive
Dubuque, IA 52004-1840

ISBN 978-0-7575-9690-2

Printed in the United States of America
10 9 8 7 6 5 4 3 2 1

Contents

♦♦♦

English as a Second Language

Freshman Composition

Sophomore Composition

The Polishing Cloth

Editorial Board

◆◆◆

Preface

"The true measure of a man is not how he behaves in moments of comfort and convenience, but how he stands at times of controversy and challenges." - Martin Luther King Jr.

The Seventeenth edition of *The Polishing Cloth* is an "open book" of ideas and creativity. Once it is opened, the diversity of power is illustrated through the art of words. As each essay is read, the audience will understand how students have captured the essence of their lives and experiences. I know that education is power, and being able to communicate with people is power. *The Polishing Cloth* gives students from every campus at Georgia Perimeter College the ability to do just that. They have not only empowered themselves, but the students in this edition want to empower others. Writing can be a challenge, yet the understanding of that challenge is measured in the words put on paper.

The Polishing Cloth, founded by Sarah Larsen in 1984, is a publication of Georgia Perimeter College that collects the best student essays from developmental studies, English as a second language, English composition, and other disciplines, complementing the textbook with accessible student models.

The success of *The Polishing Cloth* year after year is because students have the belief that they can achieve. With faculty encouraging and inspiring students to submit essays for consideration, it enables many students to have a "voice" and be heard through their words.

Family is a bond that holds the pieces of a puzzle together. The support of my husband, Adrian, has been amazing. You kept me motivated and pushed me to keep going in the most stressful times. To my two daughters, Arianne and Nasya, I am so blessed to have you both in my life. Each of you has shown me a better way to look through "my window" and enjoy it.

The Polishing Cloth continues every year with the hard work of the Editorial Board. Each semester, they have committed themselves above and beyond in reading essays. I want to personally thank each of you for your time and dedication to this literary work, students, and Georgia Perimeter College. Mike Hall, assistant editor of *The Polishing Cloth*, your sound advice and guidance helped me along the way. You have been a wonderful mentor.

Before I close, I challenge every student to look within and seek the creativity that shines. Every book has a unique cover, but it is not a book unless there is something to bring it to life.

Na Keya H. Bazemore, Editor

My Goals for the Next Five Years

Calvin Oliver
ENGL 0098

♦♦♦

The most important factor in someone's life is to create goals. In order for me to be a successful person, I must challenge myself by creating goals that I can accomplish. These goals will allow me to follow a path without becoming sidetracked. I have experienced the rewards from setting goals, and they are a necessity for me. My educational goals are first, my career goals will provide income for my family, and my personal goals will balance the other two goals.

My educational goals are very important to me. I decided to earn an Associate's degree from Georgia Perimeter College in the field I love, which is computer science. Once I accomplish my goals at GPC, I want to transfer to Kennesaw State University to work on my bachelor's degree. After I earn my computer science degree, I will go to school to become a military warrant officer. "Phew!" When all is said and done, the hardest part will be over; I will have a bachelor's degree in the field of computer science, and I will have become an officer for the United States Military.

Next are my career goals and aspirations. Since I am already employed by Delta Airlines, I will apply for a job as an IT professional with Delta. Once I lock this job in, I can move on to establishing my own inventions and company ideas. Learning the skills and techniques needed, I can easily create better goals and ideas for my computer company. My career goals will not only provide a decent life for my family; they will also provide a guideline and a path for my children.

My personal goals are never last and most definitely not the least. Throughout my life, whether I am creating goals or coming up with ideas, I will always have my personal goals to help me balance my education and career. My first personal goal is to take care of my health and well-being. I love to exercise. When I take jogs or long walks, I am building my endurance and releasing stress from my body. Eating healthy foods is another way I stay in shape and healthy. My second personal goal is to love my wife and children every day and make sure they are happy. The most important part of my life is my family; they are the bread and water of my soul. As a husband and a father, I have to be a gentlemen and a protector. As a husband, I am responsible for the stability of our home, which means paying most of the bills, cleaning our home, and helping my wife with her needs. As a father, I am responsible for providing direction for my two sons, which are six and three. As a father, I must also make sure they are loved each day by reading to them, playing games with them, and going to their Taekwondo class. When my home is balance, my life is balanced.

Goals are very important parts of our lives. If we live without them, we will live in chaos. In order to be anything in life, one must create a written outline or blueprint on how to get there. By me accomplishing my goals, I will have created a blueprint for others to follow.

***

Why I Like This Essay: This is an exemplary essay because it is successful at every level. The essay is a fine example of how to execute a traditional, five-paragraph essay; the essay includes a clear thesis, strong topic sentences, and good examples for support. The essay is also instructive for other students because Calvin is so clear about what his goals are and the steps he needs to take to reach his educational and career goals. He then demonstrates the wisdom of setting personal goals that give his life much needed balance and that emphasize the importance of his family. We would all do well to write such an articulate, balanced, and clear "blueprint" for our lives to keep us motivated and focused like Calvin.
Dr. Valerie Dotson, Associate Professor of English

Lessons from Reality Television

Joshua Brinson
ENGL 0098

◆◆◆

"Now is a good time to buy a house." That is what everyone advises me since the economy is down. People fail to remember all of the responsibilities that come with buying a home. Thanks to reality television, I have the knowledge I need to further decide when it is a good time for me to purchase a home. The lessons I have learned would prevent me from having bad experiences after I have purchased a home. Reality television has taught me how to buy a home, inspect a house, and hire a professional contractor.

One lesson I have learned from reality television is how to buy a home. The show <u>Property Virgins</u> takes first time home buyers through a step by step process of purchasing a home. First, the home buyers must get financing through a bank or a mortgage broker to dictate their price range. They also get to search for a good interest rate on their monthly payments. Second, they get to choose a location. The good neighborhoods are most likely near a good school district. Finally, the home buyers place a bid on the house they want. Sometimes, they have to negotiate on a good price from the home owner. Buying a home is a long process but is worth it at the end.

Another lesson I have learned from reality TV is how to inspect a home. For example, the show <u>Holmes Inspection</u> goes into detail on what to look for in the inspection process, like looking at the electrical to see if it is up to code. One episode showed a bathroom that had an electrical outlet placed under the vanity sink where possible water could cause a deadly electrocution. The possibility of termites is something else to look for. For example, if I see wood studs touching earth, then it is a good possibility that termites have invaded the wood. A good home inspection could prevent me from buying a lemon.

The most important lesson I have learned from reality television is how to hire a professional contractor. Just because a person says he or she is a professional does not mean it is true. For instance, the show Holmes on Homes gives a clear picture to why I should not hire just anyone to fix anything in my home. The contractors on the show fix shoddy work from bad previous contractors. Most of the work completed on the show can cost up to $100,000 easily. They may start off by fixing a leaky basement, and then they end up finding other problems, like a weak unsupported foundation and illegal junction boxes. Mike Holmes recommends asking questions until I am satisfied, looking at the previous work related to mine, and getting permits before starting any home improvements. By doing my due diligence, I can weed out the bad contractors.

I am not in a rush to purchase a home because I do not want to buy a house full of unexpected problems. I need to make the necessary money to keep up the value of my property. Right now, I feel as if there is more I need to learn from reality television. The knowledge I have now makes me more confident in protecting my investment. Otherwise, in the end, it is what I don't know behind the dry walls that can cost me a fortune.

***

Why I Like This Essay: In addition to following all of the rules of the traditional essay, this is a great learning support essay because it does a really good job of taking a fresh approach to this topic. Although many people think about the lowest common denominators when assessing the value (or lack thereof) of reality television, Joshua focused on truly beneficial reality programming. Joshua's essay demonstrates that making smart choices when we are flipping through our television programming guide can actually make us smarter people and that there are some positive, practical lessons to learn from reality television. Additionally, he uses the sophisticated approach of referencing three different, but related, reality shows that have helped him amass knowledge on one specific topic of interest, buying a home. This kind of focus in a timed, in-class essay is exemplary, and Joshua was able to deliver excellent content routinely because he took seriously the necessity of generating ideas and planning before drafting.
Dr. Valerie Dotson, Associate Professor of English

Being a Good Parent

Jasmine Eccles
ENGL 0098

Being a good parent is not as easy as it sounds. In fact, his or her role can be very overwhelming. Most new parents do not know if they are doing the right things to care for their children. Even experienced parents wonder about their decisions and children. All parents, however, try to be responsible and make the best choices they can. They try to develop characteristics that will help them to be the best possible parent. Some of these characteristics are being a good example, being a good caregiver, and being a good disciplinarian.

The first characteristic of being a good parent is being a good example. Most parents are their child's first role model. Children seem too often to learn from what their parents do and not what their parents say. For example, when parents are confident about themselves, in addition to their lives and dreams, children will often follow and be confident about themselves. Also, being successful is a good example for children because this accomplishment encourages children to go far in life and never give up. When children see their parents accomplish something, they want to do better than their parents and make their parents proud. Furthermore, good examples can start with small actions, such as grooming and table manners. When children have a model of behavior to follow rather than just instruction, they seem to take the lesson more seriously.

The second characteristic of being a good parent is being a good caregiver. For instance, one day I was getting my children ready to go, and I realized my daughter was feeling very feverish. I checked her temperature, and it was 105.6 degrees Fahrenheit. I knew at that point her temperature was too high and could cause brief seizures, brain damage, or even death if it got any higher. Immediately, I put her in a cold bath to break the fever, gathered my belongings, put the children in the car, and I drove straight to the hospital. I was so worried and scared for her, but I knew I had to do everything possible to help her. The doctors ran a number of tests on her as I held her and showed her I loved her. Our visit to the hospital was unsuccessful because the doctors could not find anything wrong with her except for the fever, so we were sent home. Days passed as I took care of all of her needs and wants until she was back to good health. Being a good caregiver is not always easy but is the most common characteristic a parent has because people always seem to care for those they love.

Finally, a good parent is a disciplinarian. Most parents discipline their children because they love and care about their future. For example, when I was younger, I was socializing in my neighborhood with a group of friends, and we noticed a new boy who had moved in a couple of doors down. This new boy saw the rest of us outside and walked over to us, but he was so rude and obnoxious that my friends and I walked away. Later that day, his parents told him to bring his things inside the house; instead, he just walked off and did not come back until everything was all unpacked. The first week after he moved into the neighborhood, he already had a bad name, and all of our parents old us to stay away from him. Not only did he not have any friends, but his lack of discipline landed him in a youth detention center. Everyone blamed the parents because he apparently had no discipline or guidance in life. His parents must have let him do whatever he wanted and never gave him any consequences for bad behavior. Discipline can change a child's outcome in life.

In conclusion, being a good parent comes with many roles. Parents who really try are never really better than others because everyone is different. There are certain qualities that parents should provide for their children, such as being a good example, caregiver, and disciplinarian. Being a good parent is not easy, yet being a parent is a worthwhile experience.

***

Why I Like This Essay: Jasmine's essay appealed to me because she used some vivid examples from her own experience as a parent and from that of other parents whom she has known, and as she progressed in this first draft, she warmed to her subject using specific language to bring it alive. Jasmine began the semester as a reluctant writer who learned the importance of paying careful attention to planning, detail, and organization, knowledge which brought her success and skill as a writer.
Mary Shelfer, Instructor of English

The Grief of Losing a Friend

Jessica Joiner
ENGL 0098

◆◆◆

Growing up in modern society having a "BFF, or best friend forever, is essential in young people today. Teenage and adolescent girls love to flaunt BFF necklaces, bracelets, and shirts to show off their friend they have deemed for life. Commonly, these friendships are made quickly and die with age. Losing a friend is always hard no matter the situations. Friendships seem to end over time due to incompatibility, jealousy and maturity.

Making a new friend is easy. People might find that they share the same interest in music or movies that make them instantly connect. Usually, that is where the similarities stop. After spending time with a friend, one may come to realize that he or she does not share the same beliefs. On the reality show Bad Girls Club, house mates Nikki and Jessica seemed to have instantly connected because they were both tomboys. That friendship ended after Nikki was unapologetic for hurting another house mate. Even today, friends may find they do not share the same morals or emotional needs. Having a friend who is messy and clumsy may find it hard to be friends with someone who is a stickler for neatness. Dealing with an opposite personality over a period of time can cause anyone to end a friendship.

Most people are highly possessive. If something is theirs, no one is allowed to touch, look, and think about that person's possession. Friends tend to do this. When a new person is introduced in their friendship, like a new partner, it can bring strain on the relationship. The person may not be jealous that the friend has a partner, but the bond that those friends shared is now being shared with someone else. On the show Sixteen and Pregnant, twin sisters seemed to have been torn apart by one of the sibling's boyfriend of whom she became pregnant by. The twin left out accused the pregnant sister of spending her time and sharing her secrets with the boyfriend only. Many may feel like this in their current friendship. They could be jealous of the fact their BFF has a partner and may feel replaced. Even one of the friends making new friends can bring tension to the relationship. Some may find this lack of coping with the issue of new relationships a lack of maturity.

A mature person can be perceived in different ways. Maturity, in this sense, means growing different priorities. Everyone is aware of the curse in high school. Friends who grew up together suddenly do not speak anymore causing a long awkwardness through the years. Suddenly, the things they may have once shared or thought of as funny diminish. One may not view the friend as mature as they are. In the movie Mean Girls, one of the characters said her friendship ended because the girl had not yet grown into a girly girl. That particular character found having boyfriends and the latest fashions as important, thus losing a friend from childhood. Other ways friendship might end because of maturity are through priorities. Priorities change when people grow up, causing friends to separate their time from each other. For example, a friend might consider getting homework done and passing all classes a priority whereas another friend may choose having fun and being dumb as a first choice. When friendship comes, opposites really don't attract.

Losing a friend is never an easy task. It hurts more because that person could have possibly been deemed a best friend forever. Friendships have many complications, but some are harder to get over than others. As people get older, their needs change. A friendship that may have been satisfactory at one point suddenly does not give the same pizzazz it once did. This annoyance can end friendships over time due to incompatibility, jealousy and maturity.

A Heart at Peace

Dericka Gale
ENGL 0099

♦♦♦

"You will never be successful! You are a loser! I wish I
had aborted you!" These were the words my mother once said to
me. I never could understand why, but the words released from
her tongue were symptoms from a sickness called schizophrenia.
My mother was a verbally abusive woman through her sickness,
but my mother could not control her illness without going
through the right treatment. Living in a home with my mother
suffering from schizophrenia was not the greatest, but I would
not change it for the world because I learned from it. However, I
gave up on my mother. I was embarrassed of her diagnosis, so I
ignored her cry for help. A child should never be ashamed of his
or her parents, but I learned that a little too late. I lost years of
getting to know my mother only wishing I would have stood by
her. I could have learned to handle my mother's sickness,
educated others who might have been dealing with the same
situation, and learned that nobody is perfect.

I speak to my mother everyday now, but six years have passed that I can never get back. I was a young child and not willing to accept that my mother was different. There were days my mother would sit on the porch and have a whole conversation by herself. This was one of her many symptoms she had suffered from. My mother would hear a voice and respond like there was really someone else in the room. I wish I could have sat by her then and let her know that everything would be alright. I could have done a lot of things to help my mother, yet I was too busy being ashamed. I cry now because my mother needed me then, and I let her down. A lot of people say a child needs his or her parents, but what about a parent needing his or her child? I was not there, and now those years are lost.

One benefit from learning about my mother's diagnosis would be educating others who have no knowledge of someone suffering from schizophrenia. I am ashamed of not taking the time out to understand what may have caused this sickness to occur. I now know that this is a rare disease, and I just was not willing to understand what was going on. I could have helped my younger siblings and prevented them from suffering too, but I only left them wondering and alone because I was too much of a coward to stay home. Educating the public about schizophrenia has now been on my daily agenda. I speak to many young adults who are living with someone suffering from this sickness. I wish I were as wise as I am now back then since I am no longer ashamed of my mother's behavior.

I also had to understand that not everyone is perfect. No one is made in the same size, shape, or color. I was judgmental because my mother was different. I treated her poorly by not standing by her side. I was embarrassed because she stood out. I should have been proud of my mother, and I should have been proud that she was strong enough to survive. My mother is a wonderful woman. My mother is a warrior, a fighter, and a true icon. She did not allow her sickness to take control of who she is. I had judged my mother from the outside looking in, but I did not take the time out to understand that my mother had suffered and survived. I never should have walked away because my mother was not perfect.

Never be a coward and run from what cannot be changed. I am not proud of my actions, but I have changed from being blinded of those who might judge others to being able to see that we are who we are because we are all different. How boring would life be if we were all the same? I took a glance in the mirror and found out what was preventing me from standing by my mother and her sickness. I was only running from myself.

***

Why I Like This Essay: In this essay, Dericka was not afraid to tell the truth. I always tell my students to reach from the inside; if anything is bothering them, I tell them to put it into writing. She not only put the blame back on herself, which is often hard to do, but she educated her audience in reference to the aspects of Schizophrenia. I could picture her mother sitting on the porch having her own conversation. This is something that many people would turn away from. Eventually, Dericka was able to come around and understand that all her mother needed was help. I admire Dericka's honesty in this essay. She truly evoked emotion in all of her readers.
Kenneth McNamara, Instructor of English

Reasons Employers Should Fire Employees

Edward Wanambwa
ENGL 0099

♦♦♦

After separating from the military, I was hired by a major telecommunications company as a Transmission Systems Manager. My responsibilities were to ensure that new and existing customers received quick and efficient resolutions to network and equipment outages. My areas of responsibility were the cities of Atlanta, Athens, and Macon, Georgia. Mt team consisted of ten field technicians, two sales engineers, and an administrative assistant. I was responsible for a very important department in the company, and my position was quite challenging and stressful. Despite my best efforts in attempting to build a good team, there were times that I was forced to fire employees. Terminating an employee is a very unpleasant, but sometimes necessary experience to deal with as an employer. I was required to fire an employee if he or she failed to perform an assigned task, failed to report to work on a timely and consistent basis, or failed to adhere to company policy.

If an employee failed to perform an assigned task, it often meant that other members of the team could not do their jobs in serving the customers. I was very diligent in ensuring that my technicians clearly understood their roles in the company and on my team. Inevitably, there were individuals who would not or could not follow simple directions. For example, I posted a list of required tools and equipment that my technicians needed to perform installs and make repairs at customers' sites. This list was distributed to every person on the team, and I even reviewed the list during weekly team meetings. Despite my efforts to make sure that my technicians were prepared to perform their assigned task, I had an individual who failed to adhere to the posted rules. He would often arrive at a customer's site ill prepared to perform his job in a timely and efficient manner. After several warnings, both verbal and written, I was forced to fire him from the company due to poor work ethic and failure to perform his job.

The second reason employers terminate employees is the failure to report to work on a timely and consistent basis. My team was required to work based on deadlines, and if a deadline is missed, the consequences not only affected my team, but the customer. If installations and equipment repairs were not completed on time, it often meant that customers would cancel their service and move to another communication provider. It was imperative that my technicians reported to work on time and arrived at their assigned customer sites on a regular basis. This is an essential part of my employee's job description. Failure to adhere to this requirement often left me with no choice but to terminate the employee. Most of my technicians were hard workers who performed their jobs well in accordance with company policy. However, for every good employee, there is an employee who tries to work the system to his or her advantage. Unfortunately, I had a few employees like that on my team. After repeated warnings about their attendance, failure to arrive to work and at customers' sites on time, I was forced to fire them. Terminating an employee's job is not easy, but as an employer, it comes with being in a leadership position.

The third reason employers have to fire employees is failure to adhere to company policy. I also had to deal with this issue as a manager. For instance, the company policy was that whenever a technician parked a truck at a customer site, the technician was required to place an orange warning cone by the front driver's side tire. This policy was put in place to protect the driver, the company vehicle, and pedestrians who might be walking by the truck. By making the driver get out of the vehicle and place the warning cone out, he or she was able to make a visual inspection of the truck and the area, thereby preventing accidents and potential injuries. I realized that this policy could sometimes be a bit cumbersome and annoying, but it was a directive passed down to me by my senior management, and it had to be enforced. After thoroughly explaining this policy to my team, I received a call from a technician at a customer site informing me that he had been involved in an accident. I arrived on site to find damage to the company vehicle and to the customer's rear office door. I immediately asked the technician if he had placed the orange warning cones in its proper place. Moreover, I asked if he had conducted a thorough inspection of the customer's site prior to moving the vehicle. After some explaining, the technician finally admitted that he had failed to follow company policy regarding the warning cone, and based on his admission, I had no choice but to let him go.

Terminating an employee is a very difficult thing to do. Something as simple as failing to place a warning cone in front of a company vehicle cost an employee his job. I might not seem fair, but by not following instructions, the employee put himself, others, and the company at risk. Not reporting to work on a timely and consistent basis is another reason employers fire employees. After all, people are paid a salary to show up on time and do their assigned tasks in a timely and efficient manner. When that fails to happen, employers are often forced to terminate that employee and hire someone who will show up and do his or her job. Company policies are often implemented for a good reason. More often than not, company polices are based on prior incidents that the company wants to avoid in the future and when an employee fails to follow these policies, it puts the company and the employee at risk. When something like this occurs, employers are sometimes forced to fire violators and reduce any liability the company might face. I realize that in this economy, jobs are important, and no employer wants to put an employee in a difficult position financially or otherwise, but by following simple rules and using common sense, many employees can avoid termination from their jobs and enjoy long and prosperous careers.

***

Why I Like This Essay: Edward's essay resonated with me because of the organization, presentation of ideas, and confident mastery of the essay form. Also, on a personal note, I thought that his poignant language evoked the hard work, effort, and love that he puts into his marriage. Seldom have I had a student in Learning Support whose writing seems so effortless as he plans and executes a nearly flawless essay on his first draft.
Mary Shelfer, Instructor of English

The Most Influential Person in My Life

Doriyana Monconduit
ENGL 0099

◆◆◆

My life was not all that great when I was living in New Orleans. I did not do well in school, and my grandmother would not help me with my school work. I was failing classes, behaving badly, and not listening. My godmother gave me a better life and has been the most influential person in my life.

My godmother has helped me get a better life. Since my parents could no longer take care of me, so my godmother took care of me. The environment that I was living in was not all that great either. There were other children living where I was, so there was not a lot of space. I would move from house to house and ended up changing schools all the time, attending five or six different elementary schools. When I moved into my godmother's house, I had my own room and bed. I did not have to share any of my things.

I received a better education while I was living with my godmother. When I stayed with my grandmother, I did not get good grades. My grandmother would not help me do any of my homework. However, my godmother would help me with my homework when I did not understand what I was doing. Since she is a math teacher, she helped me with math problems I did not understand. If I had an essay I had to do, she would read over it for any errors. She would also help me study for a test I had to take and show me what I could do to help me study for a test, like make note cards.

I did not have a good personality, so my godmother helped me. She would tell me to go out and try to make new friends so that I could meet. My godmother would teach me how to communicate with others and get to know them much better. I got over being shy while I was living with her. Furthermore, she would tell me to go and join clubs so that I could meet new people. Being on the dance team and step team at my school helped me get out and make friends.

Having someone who cares about me and is willing to make my life a better one is very helpful. If I would have never moved to Georgia, I do not think I would be where I am today. Having someone whom I could look up to is very inspiring, which is why I am thankful to have my godmother. She has influenced me more than anyone else in my family.

***

Why I Like This Essay: This essay has a clear thesis and is well-organized, but Dori has gone further by creating an emotional layer within her paper. By using very specific, personal examples, she brings us into some difficult girlhood experiences as well as a powerful relationship with her godmother. The details in this essay speak to most any reader because the examples evoke an underlying understanding of how we relate to one another.
Shellie Welch Sims, Instructor of English

Living in Different Places

Yaroslav Kuznyetsov
ENGL 0099

The majority of people who own a house tend to live there most of their life without relocating. Throughout my life, I moved around a lot, so there are quite a few places that I have called home over the years. There are a variety of previous homes that I could portray for comparison during my stay in America. As interesting as it would be to compare homes in the same country, it would be far more interesting to compare homes in two different countries. I will paint a picture of what the living conditions are like in Kiev, Ukraine versus my home here in America.

My first encounter with a place I would soon call my home was on May 7, 1992 in Kiev, Ukraine. During my stay in Kiev, I began to notice some things about the place that I lived, and those things were not at all pleasant. As I began to get bigger, the house I lived in got smaller and more uncomfortable. I should not have been surprised because it had three people living in a one bedroom condominium. Just to put it in perspective of how small the house was, the kitchen in my house was as big as a bathroom in most apartments in the U.S. Some other things that I did not notice before were the nasty corridors and elevators leading up to my house. The corridors had trash and human waste along with the elevators, so the smell was not very appealing. When I entered my building, I tried to dash as fast as I could to my house to get away from the smell. I knew that I did not like this house, but at the same time, I thought that there was not anything better.

Ten years after my stay in Kiev, I relocated to Atlanta, Georgia and settled down in some apartments called Tara Trails. Even though the apartments were not luxurious, they were well kept and big enough to hold three people unlike my house in Kiev. Instead of a one bedroom, we had a three bedroom, and everyone got his or her own room. The kitchen was huge compared to my old house; the bathrooms were at least ten times bigger, and the most amazing thing was that there were multiple bathrooms instead of just one. For the first time ever I saw a walk-in closet, and it was so big that I thought it was my room. I felt really good about having my own room and enjoyed the privacy. This house was hands down a lot better than my old house in Kiev.

The house in America was much better than my house in Kiev, but it is not the luxuries that make the house. It is the experiences and memories that I have from that place that make it. Even though my first house did not have huge bathrooms and room size closets, I still loved it because of the people who lived there and because it was where I experienced life for the first time.

The Best and the Worst Job

Sompong Liwwayha
ESL 0091

◆◆◆

When looking back at the jobs that I had in the past ten years, I was lucky enough to have good experiences. However, like many students at Georgia Perimeter College, I might like one job more than another. I have worked in three different countries: Thailand, the Netherlands, and the United states. The worst job that I had was working in the Groningen museum café in the Netherlands, and the best job that I had was working at the insurance company in Thailand.

When I graduated from Bangkok University in Thailand, I wanted to have an adventure, so I went to the Netherlands. I lived there for five-years and it was a very good experience. However, it was difficult for me to get a good job because I did not speak the Dutch language. I found a job at the Groningen Museum Café, cleaning the dishes. I am sure many people think that dishwashing is an easy job. Please trust me on this one. It was a really hard job, and you needed to be physically and mentally fit. It was hard because of two reasons: the first reason was because I had to stand seven straight hours, and it was very hot in the kitchen. It was like standing in a jail cell with no window, and all that I saw the whole day were the dirty dishes.

The second reason was because I had to put up with the stereotypes that the Dutch people had toward me. Without having good Dutch language skills, they often thought that I was an outsider and did not accept me in the group. It was hard for me to fit in.

Not only did I have a job I disliked, I had a job that I enjoyed. When I was nineteen years old, I worked with the Thai Life Insurance Company. This was the best job that I have had so far. Selling life insurance in Thailand was totally different from most of the insurance companies in the United States. I did not spend time only in my office on the phone, yet I also went outside to visit people in their homes. I liked to work and communicate with people, and this job provided me with both opportunities. I found that the way people lived was very interesting; I also learned more about my own cultural values when I talked and exchanged ideas with people who lived in small towns. Furthermore, I got a promotion and went to Malaysia for ten days while I was working with the company.

I will always make the best of any job that I have because I believe that if I work hard, I will be rewarded. I have tried to learn from my previous work experiences. I plan to make use of this knowledge when I become a nurse. I will remember my best and worst jobs.

The Best Job

Robel Teklehaimanot
ENGL 0099

Many people have different kinds of jobs. Some people like their jobs and others do not. I have a job, like most people, parking cars. It is one of my best jobs I have had in my life. The reason I like my job is because of the salary and the relationship with my coworkers.

One of the reasons that I like this job is the salary I am getting paid. Before I started working valet, my first job was as a cashier in a Publix. I was paid $7 an hour. Therefore, I was not comfortable with the job, and that is the time I started looking for another one. I did not wait for long. After two weeks, I found the job that I was looking for, which is valet at the Atlanta Ritz Carlton Hotel downtown. The first time I was shocked because I thought the salary was only $6, but I did not think about the tips. Even though the job is harder than my previous one, it is much better comparing the salary I am paid. Furthermore, sometimes if there is a function or some kind or holidays, I make more than $12 in an hour. The more people we visiting the hotel the more money I can get.

The second most important reason I like my job is the relationship with my coworkers. My manager is from the same country that I am from, which is Eritrea, and one of my best friends works there. Therefore, I feel more confident when I am working. I remember one day I had a family wedding, and the next morning I had to go to work. I knew that I could not make it, so I called one of my coworkers to cover my shift; he was so pleased. Basically, we always help each other when we have these kinds of situations.

All in all, my last three years in the United States I am very grateful for my job. In fact, I can save a lot of money, and I am can help my family with different types of bills. Therefore, I will always try to do my best to make things better.

Heat Exhaustion

Cindy Sok
ESL 0091

Having a job is a very pleasurable thing in these days because many people have lost their jobs. I have been working with my parents for two years, and this job is very stressful. Therefore, working in my parent's dry cleaners is the worst job that I have ever had in my life because it is hot in the summer, and I hate working with my parents.

I really do not like summer because of the hot weather. When I am working in the cleaners, I have to staple a name tag to customers' clothes, so I have to stand up until I finish with the tagging. The fact is that there are about 500 clothes that customers bring in to the cleaners and that is all for me to do. The cleaners get busier in the summer, so the cleaning machines are working until the business closes; therefore, the temperature in the cleaners is twice as hot as the temperature outside. Working in the cleaners is one place that I hate during the summer months.

Secondly, I hate working with my parents because it is really uncomfortable. They expect too much from me, and I have to show only a good part of me to other employees because I am the owners' daughter. Accordingly, my parents will not let me wear a hat, short pants, and t-shirt. Somehow, it could be comfortable working with some parents, but not for me. My parents will not let me have any other kind of job, and I want to have new experiences, so I told my parents that I want to have a new experience, and they are considering it now.

In conclusion, I am working at a terrible job right now. However, it is only my first job and my first experience, so who knows if maybe this job will be my best job in the future. Furthermore, I cannot wait until I get a new job and have new experiences.

Flying into Fast Food

Gabriel Diaz
ESL 0091

I am sure we have all had a job before. It is common these days to see teens working as a cashier, retailer, or simply taking orders at a restaurant. Some teens have jobs because they need it in order to cover their needs or because they want to experience something new. I have had many positive and negative experiences when I worked at a particular job. My worst job ever was at the Atlanta International Airport Hartsfield Jackson, working as a cashier for Burger King. This was also my first job, and I experienced stress and pressure as I never felt before.

Working as a cashier for Burger King at the world's busiest airport was nothing easy for me. This center inside terminal D is not just like any conventional fast food area. Inside the airport, the employees, and I had to satisfy all customer needs, but it is hard when we have to attend to not tens or hundreds, but thousands. Although I was not a native speaker, I found it easy to communicate with the customers. I was a cashier and had to take orders. Sometimes, I had to take care of the food that was coming in. I was basically doing two jobs in one. I thought to myself, "What am I doing here?"

On the other hand, I had to count the money before and after I was done for the day, something that was not easy at all. I had to memorize the menu, as well as the price according to the size of the order; all of it I had to learn in a matter of days. Also, I had to have in mind what type of payment the customer wanted to make. There were around five types of payments, and I had to be really careful because it is not permitted to use any other currency but the U. S. dollar.

Even though it was not the best job ever, I learned and experienced new things. It made me feel some joy and satisfaction when I saw customers smiling, knowing that my effort to satisfy their needs was worth it.

Meeting it the Hard Way

Abebaw Woldehana
ESL 0091

♦♦♦

     DeKalb Farmers Market was the place where I started my first career. In May 2008, I applied for a job at the DeKalb Farmers Market, and the management accepted my application and hired me as a meat cutter at the market. I was very thin and short to work at the meat department, but I accepted the opportunity to work as a meat cutter. Being a meat cutter was the worst job I had in my life because I had to work in a freezer for extended hours, and I used to deal with a very strict management team.

     The work place can make work the best or the worst. When I used to work at the DeKalb Farmers Market, I used to stay in the freezer at least for three hours once I arrived. The worst thing was I had a responsibility to conduct an inventory every morning before the meat was displayed at a counter. When I did the inventory, I did not used to wear gloves because it was not comfortable to write with the gloves. Furthermore, every item located in the freezer was frozen, so it was the worst to move items from place to place in there. It was Sunday, and nobody was with me when a roll of frozen meat accidentally dropped on my leg while I was doing weekly inventory in the freezer. The worst pain I ever had was that.

The management team of the market was the other worst thing that I faced in my first job. The team was organized from different departments and had a responsibility of following each and every activity in the market. The team was told to give a written warning whenever they saw a mistake. The team was divided into pairs and used to move around the market while employees were working. One day when I was working in the freezer, two of the management members came to me and asked why I did that particular job. I explained to them why I did that, and I was correct. Since they did not have any idea about the department, they did not accept my explanation and finally gave me a written warning.

All in all, work is the major key to open my future; therefore, I have to like it and make it the best. The best work can be achieved by hard work. I strongly recommend people to work hard and to make their job the best of all.

The Nightmare of Chop-Sticks

Quan Chen
ESL 0091

I have worked many different kinds of jobs. Some of these jobs had a really good monthly pay or a really nice boss, but many of these jobs were just stressful to me for many reasons. The worst job that I ever had in my life was working as a waiter in a Chinese restaurant called "Chop-Sticks." This was the worst job ever because the working hours were long, and the restaurant did not have enough employees.

The working hours in a Chinese restaurant are generally longer than American restaurants, but the working hours at "Chop-Sticks" were ridiculous. I had to start working from 9:00 am all the way to 11:00 pm six days a week. Doing the math, that was about fourteen hours a day and eighty-four hours a week. As a waiter, I had to stand during my job from sun rise to sun set. The only time that I was able to sit down was during the time when employees were having meals. As a result, every night when I got home, I had to put a bag of ice on my knees to make them feel better.

After I had worked at "Chop-Sticks" for about a week, my knees got used to the stress of standing for fourteen hours straight. However, the fact that the restaurant did not have enough employees kept me busy for the rest of the summer. At the beginning, the restaurant had about four waiters, but two of them left for personal reasons. Therefore, the other waiter and I had twice as much workload as before. The stress really kicked in around 6:00 p.m. because that was the time when the restaurant was the busiest. It was so busy that we were literally running to serve food on the table for the customers. By the time the restaurant got some new waiter , we did not care anymore because the summer was about to be over, and we were about to leave.

Working at "Chop-Sticks" last summer was a nightmare. I do not know if the customers sensed the eagerness of me wishing to go home, but boy, I am glad that was over. However, I did learn a positive thing during my job, and that is no matter how hard things seem to be, if I refuse to give up, then it will all be better in the end.

A Shot in the Dark and Aiming High

Demetrius Sharp
ENGL 1101

♦♦♦

"Integrity First, Service Before Self, and Excellence in All We Do" are the core values of the Air Force. My principles align with the core values, as well as the vision and mission of the Air Force. The alignment was a factor in my decision to enlist, but the primary reason I joined was the opportunity for a fresh start following the separation from my wife. I thought my motive was atypical, but after getting to know my brothers and sisters in arms, I was not the only one fleeing to the Air Force from a broken heart.

My wife and I were separated for the final time, and I did not want the temptation to return to a love gone wrong. I had to rebuild my name and provide for my children. The Air Force was not my first option, yet it was the best choice for a nearly thirty-year-old man starting over with no formal education. The Air Force stood out for a number of reasons including stability and housing. I would serve my country, and in the event of death, my children would be assisted. That was the convincing I needed to rush to the recruiter and leave before Christmas in December 2000. The Air Force allowed me a new beginning. I left my wife of eight years everything I owned except my clothes bought from a thrift store and a big screen television bought with my income tax return. I was looking forward to the adventures and challenges of the Air Force. I was especially excited about push-ups, running, and marksmanship. My previous employment at Bally's Total Fitness gave me an edge physically, and I felt marksmanship would come naturally given my childhood experience playing Duck Hunt on Nintendo. Apparently, my Duck Hunt days paid off because I would get an expert marksman ribbon from the Air Force for shooting a 9mm handgun.

I arrived in San Antonio, Texas at Lackland Air Force Base to begin basic training. Texas was the furthest west I had been, and it was much colder than I expected. I was twenty-seven which required an age waiver for enlistment. Our duties in basic were both physical and mentally challenging. I was prepared to compete in any physical challenge; however, I neglected to prepare myself mentally for what the Air Force had in store. The brisk cold made marching and standing in place for hours harsh. I woke at 4:00 a.m. and ate breakfast in less than five minutes. The procedures in the cafeteria were head forward, tray in front, step to the right, and move without looking forward or behind. I faced disciplinary action if I did not maintain military bearing. Once I sat down, I had to wait for three other trainees to arrive to their side of the table for four. We nervously made eye contact signaling to each other it was safe to attack our meals. I can still smell the Texas toast I ate everyday because it could be eaten hastily. After our quick bite, I rushed to formation for the barrage of questions aimed at my weakened, sleepless mind. I had a pleasant march singing cadence to our testing facility where I would take a series of multiple choice tests. This march would be one of the most peaceful times of my day. Ironically, before I enlisted, marching happened to be one of my biggest concerns about basic training. It made me nervous because everyone steps in sync, and I thought I would be the one to throw it off and become the eyesore in my drill sergeant's peripheral.

My basic training comrades and I parted ways after an emotional graduation. We had a send-off graduation party, which consisted of heavy drinking and chasing women, stereotypical military male behavior. When I arrived at my next duty station in Biloxi, Mississippi at Keesler Air Force Base to attend tech school, I felt more assured of how things would operate. I felt more comfortable discovering my new surroundings, but flashbacks of basic training haunted me on occasion. At tech school, I still had tight rules, but it was a lot more relaxed. I stayed at tech school longer than expected due to the needs of the Air Force. The Air Force held the right to change my job and retract the bonus I was promised. These are rules enlistees abide by when they sign-up for military service. One of the core values of the Air Force is "Service Before Self," so I respected this principle and moved on to my next task. I enjoyed the convenience of living on base where everything was within walking distance. I purchased goods at the local market and walked freely as long as I maintained military etiquette. I formed an alliance with another Airman named Ralin. We shared tips and tricks on how to pass tests and evaluations. Our duo grew to a pack of eight guys who watched out for each other while we trained for our permanent duty stations. Saturdays started with an early morning workout, a trip to the mall, and a stop by the beach. Saturdays ended with getting a motel, attending a nightclub, and gambling at a casino. Some weekends were spent taking a two hour drive to Bourbon Street in New Orleans, and some weekends were spent taking a morning drive to Pensacola, Florida. We had some of our best times together, and if one person needed something, the other brothers would ensure he got it. It is sad we no longer keep in contact, and the only phone number I have is for Lalo, who now lives in San Francisco. These guys would not be the only close friendships I formed along the way.

After about a year, I was assigned to my permanent duty station in Camp Springs, Maryland at Andrews Air Force Base. Now at my third duty station, I was beginning to understand how relocating frequently as a job requirement can be taxing. On the bright side, a new base meant new impressions and new friends. I was excited to be living near the nation's capital even though it was under the shadow of the September 11 attacks. I worked in military personnel maintaining records, which I found enjoyable. My job did not get overwhelming until I had to work guard duty to police the base because of Post 9/11 paranoia. To make matters worse, there was a serial killer on the loose shooting random people with a sniper rifle. The gas station on base was crowded because the D.C. Sniper shot most victims while they pumped gas. It was a stressful time, and I also felt guilty for not being able to see my kids more often. The reasons included extra workload and no one to watch my children when I went to work. I was not the only one alone. Alcohol and drug abuse was rampant on the air force base due to widespread depression and loneliness among Airmen. When individuals are brought to the Air Force from around the world, they are bound to get homesick and that makes the spirit vulnerable.

Despite a few negatives, the Air Force is an excellent place for a young adult to develop character and gain a foundation. I appreciate all the valuable training acquired because I can push myself to the limit. Enlisting in the Air Force allowed me to make lifelong friends, taught me communication skills to apply in the workforce, and provided me the G. I. Bill to attend college. In my family, a college education is somewhat rare. There are numerous benefits servicemen and women are entitled for honorable service. After leaving the Air Force, I suffered a few medical conditions that the Veteran's Administration gladly addressed. A number of VA organizations are available for my academic, medical, and financial needs. I have an advantage buying my first home and starting a business. I proudly wore a respected uniform and served my country knowing all military personnel are connected. It is a military brotherhood that I am proud to be a part.

***

Why I Like This Essay: The student's challenge here was that he wished to write about a period of his life spanning several years. Given this difficulty, the student does an excellent job in narrowing the scope of this piece. A few sentences of backstory in the introduction work well; the introduction propels the reader into the narrative with just enough information about the protagonist's past. Another strength of this essay is that each scene is developed with wonderful detail and clarity. The writer avoids relying on clichés and instead provides his own personal, specific observations and experiences. Additionally, the writer uses solid transitions to move seamlessly between places and times in the narrative. This narrative is detailed, thoughtful, and while it portrays a positive experience it avoids becoming overly sentimental.

Amber Brooks, Instructor of English

Slipping into Darkness

Bryce Monaco
ENGL 1101

September 19th, 1990, forever changed my life. I call it my own personal doomsday. This was the day I tried to take my life, yet it seemed life had other plans for me. I awoke to the sun seeping in through the blinds; it was a Wednesday. A cold breeze filled the room from an open window, leaving me cold. As I reached to turn off my radio that I always fell asleep to at night, strange feelings came over me. Something in me did not quite feel right today. I pulled myself out of bed to walk into the living room, and I turned on the TV; it was an old western. The first words spoken by the actor were, "It's a good day to die." I immediately turned the TV off. Those words just seemed to echo in my head; it was like being in a tunnel, and all I could hear were those words.

I sat on the oriental carpet in the living room that my mother had just spent twenty thousand dollars on. It was mostly blue, with cream, and little hints of red throughout it. She loved that ungodly rug. As I sat there, my mind started to race about all of the things that had gone wrong in my life. I knew who I was inside, but I also knew that society would not accept me. I just kept going back to the words I heard on the TV: "It's a good day to die." Before I knew it, I was in my mother's and step-father's bedroom. The smell of dirty sheets and sex filled the air. I hated going into their room, and more than that, I hated them. My step-father loved guns; he had his own arsenal throughout the house. He kept most of his guns in his bedroom closet along with his most valuable coins. The closet door was open. I sat at the opening of the door so that I could look at all of the guns. He had ten rifles and two pistols. The guns and the closet smelled of oil and metal. Next to the guns were coffee cans, piled on top of one another filled with silver dollars. I saw a 44 magnum revolver next to one of the coffee cans, and I slowly picked it up.

The gun was so large that it weighed my hand down when I lifted it up. It was very cold and stiff…just like a corpse. A light went off in my head; this would be the tool I would use to end all of my pain.

With the gun in my hand, I went back into my bedroom to grab my lucky batting gloves. My life was all about baseball, and I wanted something that gave me a sense of security in that moment. As I put the gloves on for the last time, I felt how soft the leather was against my skin. It was as if I smelled the ball field that I played on for so many years. If I was going to turn back, this would have been the moment. There was no turning back. I found myself in the hallway that intersected with the kitchen, bathroom, living room, and my mother's bedroom. My mind was racing at the speed of light. I put the gun to my head, and all I could think about was my grandmother seeing my brains splattered against the wall. I quickly pulled the gun back down to my side. As I pulled the hammer back on the gun, the trigger looked odd to me for some reason. Yes, it fired. From that moment, everything seemed like it was in slow motion, even my voice. It was like someone slowed down a movie, and time just seemed to halt. What was shocking is that I was still alive; my doomsday had just begun.

The room was spinning all around me as I was trying to grasp what I had just done. Then, I realized I was still alive. The gun was still in my hand. I did not know what to do with it, so I threw it forward; it landed in a pile of dirty socks in my mother's bedroom. My legs went out from underneath me, and I fell to the floor. I lifted up my shirt to see a black hole in my stomach where the bullet entered. When I reached around to my back, it was warm and wet like a hot fudge sundae. In this moment, I knew I was in trouble, and I needed help. With every ounce of strength in me, I pulled myself to the living room to call 911. Once I reached the telephone, the room started to spin. I could not think straight, and everything seemed out of order. As I picked up the telephone receiver, I found myself angered because I could not remember the number to 911! It took me a minute, but I finally was able to dial the number. A voice came on the line and I just yelled, "I've been shot!" Then, I realized I was going to be in a whole lot of trouble. I put the phone down and I looked at my hands; I still had my batting gloves on. In a panic, I pulled the oriental carpet back not to get any blood on it and pulled myself to the bedroom. When I got close enough to my room, I ripped off the gloves and threw them as far as I could into my room. Just after that, the police arrived. They put an oxygen mask on my face, plastic bags around my hands, and put me onto a gurney. Before I knew what happened, I was put in an ambulance, then on a helicopter, and finally I was in the hospital. I spent six hours in surgery and was very lucky to be alive; the bullet missed every vital organ by a hair.

September 19th, 1990, was my doomsday; it was the day I slipped into darkness and survived. Every day I look in the mirror, I am reminded of that day with the scars it left behind. It is an experience that has added both shape and texture to my life. It was a short, sweet dance with the devil, and I won.

***

Why I Like This Essay: Bryce paints a picture through words in this essay. He uses the senses in a way that a reader would not expect to see in a typical ENGL 1101 Narrative/Descriptive essay. As a reader, I felt his pain. This essay proves that writing can become a sense of therapy. Bryce was not afraid to write about something so personal. When he shared this essay with his classmates, they were completely moved by its sincerity and heart filled words. Bryce continues to give motivational speeches on teen depression and the consequences it may have. He is proud to help out anyone in need, and this came through extremely vividly through his writing.
Kenneth McNamara, Instructor of English

Childhood Memories

Alexandra Van de Water
ENGL 1101
♦♦♦

    The bell rings. I gather my things and walk out of the classroom. Along the way out of school, I swing by my little sister's classroom and wait patiently for her to waddle over, her wire rimmed glasses falling down her chubby little face as she struggles to carry her things. I swing her bag over my shoulder and wrap my arms around her, guiding her through the crowd and out into the courtyard. As we walk the short block to our house, I ask about her day. She begins to tell me every intimate little detail of her day in second grade, and while I am feigning interest, the day's chores are flowing through my brain. Did I remember to run the dishwasher this morning? What laundry is there to do? I glance down at Hannah and notice she spilled some sort of red liquid on her white uniform shirt. I almost yell at her, but she is looking at me, her crooked teeth grinning back up at me, eyebrows raised, innocently waiting for a response. I smile and smooth down her short, brown, hair, asking her to tell me again.

    Walking up the front steps, I can already hear the dogs barking. I glance behind me around to the driveway, looking for my mom's red minivan. She is not home; nothing unusual there. I let out a heavy sigh as I drop my bag at the front door, fishing through the various papers and binders for my keys. Hannah has already run off into the yard, climbing her favorite tree, searching for lizards or any other creepy crawly things she can get her little hands on. I called her name, bringing her back into reality and ushering her into the door. I walk through the foyer, the dogs jumping all over my legs, begging me to open the sliding glass door. I stop for a second to sit on the floor, letting them climb all over me, greeting me in their own special way. I glance back at the clock above the refrigerators and realize it is already 4:00 p.m. I mutter profanities under my breath, hoping Hannah does not hear me. I let the dogs out and call out to Hannah.

"Hannah! Do you want a snack?" I yell.

I wait patiently for a response and am greeted with silence. Instead of screaming again, I stomp over to her bedroom door and find her sitting in her room playing with her most treasured possessions: an eclectic mix of dinosaurs, special rocks, seashells, puppies, horses, and little paper dolls. I watch her for a moment, immersed in the story she is creating in her head. She looks so peaceful and carefree; for a second, I am overcome with intense jealousy, but then, she notices me. She glances up, not at all embarrassed for me to find her in such a personal state of mind. I ask her again if she would like something to eat. Instead of responding, she follows me into the kitchen, props herself up on the counter top, and waits patiently for me to set up her favorite snack – an entire package of soft baked, chips ahoy chocolate chip cookies and a tall glass of ice cold milk. I bring it into the family room and turn on the TV to Cartoon Network. She sits on the floor, maybe a foot away from the screen, head tilted up and eyes wide, soaking it all in. I scoot her back a little, tell her for the hundredth time to sit further away from the TV, and walk off to start the day's long list of To-Do's. I start in the kitchen. I did indeed forget to run the dishwasher, and the sink is full of the morning's dishes, now encrusted with whatever meals my mom decided to make herself. I fill the sink with water and start to scrub, hand washing a full load while the dishwasher hums beside me.

As 4:45 ticks away, I am moving on to the laundry room. I stuff white garments into the washing machine and place a load of colors into the dryer. Now, it is 6:00 p.m. Mom called an hour ago to tell me she would be home by 7:30, and she wants burgers for dinner. I climb onto a chair and reach into the freezer for the frozen Bubba Burgers. As I set everything up and begin to cook, the day's events begin to blur in my mind. Do I have homework? Did I finish my class work? My eyes begin to feel heavy-I can feel the bags beginning to form, and my arms are hanging like massive weights from my small shoulders. The clock ticks to 7:00 as I begin to set the table. I get Hannah out of Cartoon Network world and my mom's glass of wine poured. The door opens, and my mother comes in, her face set with lines of frustration. She whisks past me and into her office. I stand there, frozen in a moment of complete disappointment, but also in a state of complete numbness. There is nothing unusual about this greeting, and yet every time it hits me like a wrecking ball. I swallow whatever feelings were welling up in my chest, sit down, and begin to eat. Fifteen minutes pass and out comes my mom with a bright smile on her face, phone attached to her ear, and the latest beau filling her voids with his words. Hannah and I eat in silence, staring down at our plates. Another ten minutes pass and she finally hangs up. Looking at both of us, she says cheerfully, "Well, girls, how was your day?"

***

Why I Like This Essay: In her essay, Alexandra shows rather than tells her readers what she wants them to understand. I can see the poignancy of little Hannah alone in her bedroom surrounded by that odd assortment of playthings; I can smell the dreary everydayness of those dirty dishes piled in the kitchen sink; and I can hear the heartbreaking disconnect between mother and daughter in that voicemail message. Details like

these resonate with meanings that go beyond the words on the page. Only the best writers know how to do this.
Richard Diguette, Instructor of English

A Natural Reaction

Nathan Ellison
ENGL 1101
♦♦♦

I was ten years old when I made one of the biggest decisions of my life. My family, my cousins, and I were on vacation at Smith Mountain Lake in Virginia. We stayed in a spacious mountain-style log home. Stone stairs led from the back porch down to the lake. There was a fire pit off to the right where we roasted marshmallows and made s'mores, and to the left, there were colorful flowers and plants. At the lake, the shoreline was littered with leaves and sticks that had fallen from the trees and had been washed into the water. The leaves were grimy and slippery and the sticks jabbed at our toes as we waded in. For the most part, we avoided the shallows and jumped off the dock and plunged into the water instead. The dock was the focal point of the activities. It was just a large, ordinary wooden dock, but it provided all of the fun that we needed. We would jump off the large dock and swim to another, much smaller dock over and over again. Little did I know that this is the setting in which I would make a split-second decision that would have a profound effect on me and my family.

It was early evening. The sun was setting, and the calm lake was gently splashing against the dock. Fresh from our showers, my youngest brother, Zach, my older cousin, Brian, and I asked our parents if we could play on the dock before dinner. They said yes, and we excitedly grabbed a bottle of bubbles and ran down to the dock. My cousin Brian led the way. He was wearing a tee shirt and athletic shorts. His hair was still damp from the shower, and he was running in his bare feet. I came next. I had on a tee shirt and khaki shorts. My hair was damp, and my feet were bare, too. Last came my little brother Zach. Zach was only three years old. My mom had just given him a bath and he was running as fast as he could to keep up with my cousin and me. His hair was neatly combed, and he was wearing a tee shirt and khaki shorts. He had the biggest smile on his face as he ran after us to the dock in his bare feet.

Once we reached the dock, which was still quite warm from being bathed in the sun all day, my cousin opened up the bottle of bubbles and blew bubble after bubble of all different sizes. We began to eagerly pop the bubbles, jumping up and down with enjoyment as they burst with a touch. After a couple minutes, my mom came outside to watch us. She laughed as we pranced around like gazelles. My brother was fascinated by the bubbles. He would stand there watching a bubble with amazement, then, when the bubble got into his reach, he would hop up, pop it and clap and giggle with glee. It felt like we could have gone on for hours. We did not want to stop until the unexpected happened. Brian and I were blowing bubbles on the right side of the dock when a bubble broke off from the bunch and floated towards the left side of the dock. Zach chased after the bubble with delighted determination. He was so focused on the bubble that he did not look where he was going. I turned around just in time to catch a glimpse of my brother taking a step off the dock and falling into the lake with a splash. Without a second to think, I immediately plunged in after him since he did not know how to swim. I grasped onto him and kicked for the surface. After we reached the surface, I yelled for my cousin. Brian grabbed hold of Zach's arm and hoisted him to safety. Only then did I realize the rush of adrenaline had neutralized the water's chill.

My mom came running over to comfort my little brother. He was shocked. He didn't even realize what had happened to him. All he knew was that he was soaking wet. As my mom consoled my stunned little brother, I pulled myself out of the water. My clothes were drenched when I walked into the house. The rest of my family was bewildered. Why was I soaking wet when I had just taken a shower? They were astonished when I told them what happened.

As I was drying off, I thought about how I reacted to the situation. I realized that I had had no time to think and that it was a natural reaction for me to jump in after my brother. As my cousin described it to me, he said, "All I know is that I heard a splash and before I even turned halfway around, I heard a second splash." Later, my mom told me that I had reacted so fast that she did not even know what had happened until after my brother was back out of the water in my cousin's arms. I was so proud of myself. I had never had to react to a situation like this one, but I was especially pleased with how I had handled it. It made me very happy to know that my brother was fine, and he was still with me.

At the dinner table, I was the subject of talk. My family congratulated me for my heroic effort. I enjoyed the praise while it lasted, but stayed humble. After dinner, we went outside to have our dessert. It was a beautiful night with a full moon gleaming on the lake and through the trees. The lake was still gently splashing against the dock, and tiny waves were calmly rolling onto the shore. My dad told the children to gather twigs and small branches for a fire. We all scampered through the trees for dry wood. When we had collected enough wood, my dad lit the timber. After a few minutes, the fire was blazing, and we were ready to roast marshmallows. We grabbed some graham crackers and Hershey's chocolate bars and sat in chairs around the fire. Everyone started roasting his or her marshmallows to a golden brown. Then, all of us made our s'mores. I still remember the gooey goodness of the s'mores and our chocolate-covered faces from the melting Hersey's bars.

Everything had been restored. My brother was cheerfully running around, completely content. His face was sticky from the gummy marshmallows and the dripping chocolate. He ran around and around the fire pit until he wore himself out. He then crawled into my mom's lap and fell asleep. It was both comforting and satisfying to see him ecstatically running around with a huge smile and a constant laugh before crashing in Mom's lap. Everyone else was talking and laughing and enjoying s'mores. The glimmer of the fire and the moon lit up the faces of my family. Each face had an expression of delight and cheerfulness that was reflected by the fire's red glow.

Not another word was said about my action today, but I was satisfied nonetheless.

The eventful day was coming to a close. The luminescent moon was now high in the sky. The ground, the trees, and the water were tinted a silvery blue. The fire was dying, and the cheerfulness of the faces was fading. The youngest were already fast asleep in bed, and my cousin and I were right on their heels. With a faint smile still on my lips, I climbed into my comfortable bed and drifted off to sleep knowing that my reaction could well have saved my brother's life.

Today, the memory of all that happened that day has been extremely important to my family and me and will be for the rest of our lives. My little brother is tremendously thankful even though he cannot recount a single detail. I cannot imagine what it would have been like to lose my little brother and for him to not be in my life today. When I think back, I am amazed - and even a bit surprised - at how I handled myself. Sometimes, I can hardly believe that I acted on impulse and jumped into the water to save my little brother at such a young age. It remains my most vivid and cherished memory.

Our vacations with our cousins are very special because we do not get to see them too often. Family is extremely important to me, and we try to create many lasting, memorable moments in the precious little time that we get to spend together. I am grateful and proud that, at Smith Mountain Lake, I created a positive memory rather than one that would have overshadowed future vacations.

The Wooden Whore

Kelly Hill Hall
ENGL 1101

♦♦♦

"Sometimes you want to give up the guitar, you'll hate the guitar. But if you stick with it, you're gonna be rewarded."
- Jimi Hendrix

My acoustic guitar sits impatiently next to me while I write this paper, waiting for me to pick her up, embrace her wooden body and fondle her strings. Or, perhaps place her in a soft, black velvet case and take her on a journey to where I might show her off. Then, we can dance our harmonious dance, playing, singing, feeding off one another physically and soundly.

Throughout the ages, the guitar has often been called: an axe, six-string or plank, or given personal names. However, I have never given this acoustic guitar a name. I have only named one guitar in my life; it was a classical guitar with slick soft nylon strings, which I called *Katerina*, a Spanish name because I played flamenco style music on her mostly. Sadly, she was stolen right in front of my eyes, and it broke my heart. I vowed never again to name another guitar or give it such a characteristic of mortality. However, she is not the wooden maiden this story is about. From here on out, we will refer to my guitar in question simply as she, her, my lady or the wooden whore. Why the wooden whore? Well, she goes with me virtually everywhere; I use her to make money, and I allow drunken idiots to finger her in local pubs.

Years ago when I first walked through the doors of that small shop in Atlanta, she caught my eye immediately with her short stature, flat finish and beautiful sunburst color. Her full, perfectly curved acoustic wooden body had an alluring scent which smelled of a sensual Sitka spruce. Upon further inspection, she was uniquely branded on her head-stock in what looked like gold, spelling "Larrive`e." She felt so unadulterated in my hands and her voice was rich, bold and with soul like Aretha Franklin or June Carter. Her nickel-wound strings resonated radiantly throughout her wooden body. I knew then and there she was for me. She had other suitors as I was told by the merchant, yet I am the one she went home with.

I was at the start of a new journey in my life. As in all blossoming relationships, we were inseparable at first. Like bringing a cute puppy to a park, she would be my female ambassador, helping me break the ice with the ladies. Never jealous and always willing to show off her own goods, she knew I would never leave her behind. Over the years, our relationship grew together with the good and the bad: a multitude of broken strings, minor repairs, bloody fingers, and sweaty hands. Even knowing that I had a harem of other wooden ladies all with their own unique qualities, she was queen and received more attention than the others until one day I was summoned away to another crew that did not require her soulful sound, rather a rougher, more edgy, electric tonality, like that of Joan Jett. I set her by the wayside and began an affair with older, more experienced electric ladies, with whom I played back in the days of my youth. One was an electric blue Gibson SG with a thin sleek body and personality like Cyndi Lauper. The other, a Gibson Les Paul, coincidentally was my first love and oldest lady: pitch black in color, solid and voluptuous in shape and sound, a classic like Marilyn Monroe. My wooden lady was not bitter as far as I know. She wanted what was best for me, and I still needed her.

My life was loud and completely encompassed with this new crew. Four years passed, and occasionally my wooden lady would make an appearance and help me in my creative endeavors. At times, she would travel with me to the beach. There, with my toes in the sand, we briefly rekindled our love affair and escaped the harsh screaming tones of my electric life. I missed the honest purity of her voice and how easy she was to work with. Finally, the time came when she was required. There in the studio, her voice soulfully sang and brought a life and fullness to my crew's album that everyone around noticed and complimented. Soon after this, the world (or I should say, the greater metro Atlanta area) would know her face. An opportunity was presented to my crew in which only acoustic instruments would be allowed. This voyage would present a vast amount of exposure and that is what every crew needs. Unanimously, the crew agreed to plunge forth and play acoustically. Her big moment was just ahead. On June 4th, my wooden lady joined the crew and me as we performed live on Fox 5 News Atlanta's morning show. Together, she and I shared our fifteen minutes of fame, and she did wonderfully. However, the crews end was near. It was a tragic and unfortunately common tale: the crew split and abandoned our musical relationship leaving me alone…but not entirely.

The proverbial doors were closing around me professionally and personally. What once was a growing empire now lay in ruin. Here I was, left adrift in a sea of negativity, but there she was, keeping me afloat. My wooden lady and I played on as she nurtured and gave shape to my new voice, throwing overboard all harsh words and feelings, and redirecting this energy powering me forward to a new conquest. Family and friends by my side, it was time for me to take control of my own destiny. The time had come for us to command our own financial and artistic fate, and only she could venture forth and provide the support I would need. Luckily, a friend would come to us with a job proposal, running an open-mic at a local watering hole once a week. We graciously accepted ... and so it went.

She and I worked furiously learning songs and exploring each other's boundaries. I let her sweet tones guide my voice and her wooden body be a buffer between me and the audience, for music is my language, and she is my translator, becoming the bridge between our worlds. A steady paycheck was a welcomed addition to our adventure keeping us focused and refining our skills. The addition of songs to our repertoire brought more work, sending my wooden lady and me out into the local dives, hungry for treasure, and acceptance. We continued at this pace for two years, performing and writing, constantly sharpening our abilities. I soon noticed it was starting to wear her down physically, though her voice still rang true. Sadly, with my need to lend her body away to so many strangers' hands during the years of open-mic nights, it seemed our relationship was becoming abusive. However, even with scars and blemishes, she holds strong and sounds more beautiful than the day we met. The abuse she receives physically is overshadowed by the amount of love I have for her. I hope we will grow old together, and I can pass her on to the next lucky soul, and then the next. She will go on for generations after me until her wooden body rots away and her metal corrodes, sending her slowly crumbling back to the earth.

Some people believe that one can be at peace on this Earth without need of material things. My guitar is an extension of my existence. My beloved companion came to me via the past growing from seed to tree, over three-hundred years in the making. In some ways, she helps define me as a person and brings the music out from my soul into the air-waves for others to hear and feel. She is a material thing I would not want to live without. Why the wooden whore? Frankly, she is no whore; she is no plank; she is my soul mate, traveling through my life, sailing beside me discovering music's rewards. Maybe one day audiences will meet and be witness to the sweet siren call of my wooden lady, my acoustic companion, my guitar, my love.

The Ghetto

Alberta Jones
ENGL 1101

♦♦♦

    Some say that growing up in the ghetto, one is predestined for a terrible fate. Success is nowhere to be seen. Instead, all one sees is the destitution, despair, and anguish on the faces of babies, cousins, aunts, mothers, and sisters who could think of a better place outside the broken fenced community. This is a place where children are forbidden to play outside in their own yards for fear of being killed by stray bullets that could go off at any given moment. It is a community filled with so much ammunition; a person thinks of the Iraq war. This place is now known for its persistent drug addicts' openness to beg for spare change for their next high.

    Step after step, there is nothing but empty beer cans, dirty diapers, broken glass, used syringe needles, nothing but trash on top of trash, not a patch of green grass to be seen. Residents hear constant cursing and fighting from boyfriends and girlfriends from door to door, moaning and groaning from the elderly probably in need of healthcare, and the most disturbing of all, the innocent cries of little ones just wanting something to soothe the hunger pains. The stench of filth, which immediately overtakes someone, is like rotten remains of dead animals, feces, and urine. Although this is not a third world country, it makes one question, "Is this America, land of the free and home of the Brave?" As people walk down the sidewalks, seeing door after door without screens to protect what little humanity and dignity that is left, they are overtaken by a feeling of total grief and sadness. It seems like the only thing left are uneducated and unskilled individuals staring out, looking for a ray of hope, a savior, or a messiah to take all the pain away.

This devastating grip of poverty, which has affected this community, is a scene that is nothing less than hopeless. Is it possible for the inside to be worse than the outside? One would think not, but it is. Some of the same mothers who were just on the corner begging for money have now gone inside. One is so high that she has no idea that her three tender age children have not eaten in about a day and a half. She is clueless to the fact that she is at risk of losing them to the state. While she has been on crack for the past seven years, her future seems bleak. The baby's daddy is there sprawled out on a pissed out couch, drunk, busted, and disgusted without any drive to attempt to look for a job; he knows that finding a job will end the welfare check. He seems content with spending the money that taxpayers have provided for the household. Roaches, ants, and flies have taken up permanent residency and act like part of the family.

Hours after her high has faded, she finally realizes that she too is starving. Her desire is not for drugs at this particular moment, but for something as simple as government cheese and crackers. As she awkwardly stumbles down stairs to make her way to the kitchen, where the appliances haven't been touched in ages, she hears the pitter patter of little feet behind her. She has not realized that her kids' faces lit up like fireworks on the fourth of July as she made her way through the living room. "Come on kids, let's get something to eat," she says. As puzzled as they are, they follow her, for they know there is no such thing as a food Fairy, who comes in the middle of the day, secretively and mysteriously and fill the refrigerator and cabinets with delicious and tasty treats. Staring inside the dark cold refrigerator with nothing but a jug of water and cans of Bud light, she is struck with that feeling of guilt and shame. She realizes that she has let her kids down by trading food stamps for drugs, yet again. As she desperately tries to pacify the situation, she assures her screaming hungry children that she is only going out to get food. The cycle begins to repeat itself as she hands it to the next generation, her own blood flowing into it.

What can people do to escape this hell here on earth? Is there something better than this dreadful place, or is this their sanctuary? Are they at peace with the drive-bys, prostitution, crack houses, babies having babies, drug dealers, neglected children, and filth? Have they become so complacent that the mere thought of a better place frightens them? Or have they convinced themselves that this place is not the Ghetto, but a kind of "heaven sent" government–run facility. Yes, "Housing Project" sounds better than "the Ghetto;" still, it is one and the same. To the outside world, the Ghetto 's principle feature is a de-humanizing poverty trap, a magnet for gloom, misery, and unhappiness. To the people living inside, this place is home

Caity

Julianna Casabonne
ENGL 1101

♦♦♦

      The announcer yells out over the megaphone, "next race 19 and under girls 50 free." Five girls step up onto the block while one girl waddles up beside it. Standing beside the block, it is obvious that this girl is not like the other swimmers. Her sandy, brown hair is coming out of all sides underneath her swim cap. Her goggles have little pink dolphins on them, and her suit does not fit correctly; it pulls at her stomach and barely fits over her chest. It is clear she does not have the body of a swimmer; she is pudgier than the other girls, but she stands with her head held high with her chubby little arms by her side. Unlike the other girls who are seriously concentrating, she has a smile on her face. The crowd cries her name, "Caity, Caity!"as the swimmers take their stance to begin.

Caity does not dive into the water like all the other swimmers; she does not even bother to put her arms in a stream line. She just does an awkward cannonball into the water before the whistle even blows. The announcer says, "swimmers take your mark go!" and the whistle sounds. The other swimmers take off, but Caity just smiles and puts her head under the water and begins her slow free-style down the lane.

Every once in a while, Caity lifts her head to make sure everyone is watching and smiles and waves at her onlookers. She grabs onto the lane rope to pull herself when she is tired and does not care that she is dead last in the race. Her stroke is not smooth like the other swimmers; she lifts her head up to breath instead of to the side as she slaps the water with her hands and feet. She struggles to keep her head above the water and coughs because her mouth is still open in a smile. Caity may be slow, but she doesn't stop until she reaches the wall, and neither does the cheering of the crowd.

Once at the wall, she turns around and pushes off instead of doing a flip-turn and begins her slow journey back. By this time, the other swimmers are already finished and wait in the water for her to finish. They do not laugh at Caity, but look in admiration and loudly cheer her on with the rest of the crowd. Both teams scream words of encouragement as Caity struggles to finish her lap.

When she finally reaches the wall, she turns and hugs all the other swimmers in the pool, her smile beaming across the pool. Then, she pulls herself out of the water inch by inch until one of the two coaches reaches down to pull her out. Once out of the water, she turns around and waves at the crowd, then slowly walks over to where her mom is sitting and exclaims, "Momma, I was like a mermaid in the water!" Her mom replies, "yes, Caity, you really were; now, here's your towel. Go get ready for your next race." Caity toddles back to her chair wrapped up in a Barbie blanket high fiving every person in sight.

For all the other swimmers at the meet, a 50 free is the easiest event, but for Caity, it takes every ounce of energy she has. That iss how things have always been for her; she cannot do anything the other nineteen year old girls can. Tying her shoes takes her an hour, and picture books fill the shelves of her room.

She can only write a few words and can read only her name. While most girls her age spend their time out on the weekends partying, Caity spends her time watching The Disney Channel and playing with her Barbie dolls.

Some people look at Caity and think she is blissfully unaware of her disabilities, but in fact it is quite the opposite. Caity was born with Downs Syndrome while her twin brother Corbin was not. All of her, life she has had to watch as her brother went out and did all the things she will be never be able to do. The summer of her fifteenth birthday, Caity watched as Corbin got behind the wheel and learned that she would never be allowed to do the same. On her sixteenth birthday, she received a Barbie car while Corbin got a new white Volvo.

If asked, Caity will often say that someday she will be allowed to get her license once she learns to read better, or she will say, "I'm gradutatin from school this May. After my birthday, I'm gonna go to college with Corbin." The truth is she will not graduate until she is 21 and will never go to college. Caity was dealt an unfair hand in the game of life, but her optimism makes the game worth playing.

This past summer, I "babysat" Caity from 10 to 3 every day, and I can honestly say those days are some of the funniest of my life. The day would start with me driving to Caity's house to pick her up where I would usually find her sitting at the kitchen counter with nothing but a t-shirt on with a plate set in front of her with the most random food combinations. There would be cheerios with bananas, a fudge Popsicle with gold fish, or a peanut butter and jelly sandwich with gummies inside. Looking at her food, it was evident that Caity made her own breakfast, and she was always proud to tell me of her latest invention. She would always offer me a taste which I would politely refuse.

After Caity finished her breakfast, she would take me upstairs where she would show me her latest page in her coloring book that she had finished. The pages never had the coloring inside the lines or colors that made sense; the sky was usually pink, and the grass purple, but nevertheless, Caity was always proud of the page. She would always "sign" her pages with her name in writing that looked like that of a kindergartner's. Then,

Caity would struggle to put on her swim suit, grab either her Cinderella or Barbie towel, and slide on her goggles with the pink dolphins on the front. Finally, she would then kiss her stuffed animals good bye, and together, we would go get in my car to drive to the pool.

Once at the pool, Caity would slowly unbuckle her seatbelt, open the door of the car and scream an excited hello to the lifeguards. They would respond with a "hey Caity!" To which she replied, "hay is for horses." Laughing, she would then put her towel down, waddle to the edge of the pool, do an awkward cannonball into the water and begin her slow freestyle with a huge smile on her face.

Alchemy

Melanie McElroy
ENGL 1101

♦♦♦

Slip into a forgotten era when fire prohibition was in full effect, and the frigid masses were forced underground to seek heat. Gathering in a cavernous speakeasy, where the bootlegged fire boils the blood and inflames the desires of all who enter, you come for an evening of sanctuary, dancing and illicit fire with seductive performances by the denizens of this fire cabaret. The forces of the unknown, the effervescent spark of curiosity and the spectacle of unbridled romance with the flame; how could you deny a peek? Your mind is the only obstacle upon entering, and you may as well check it at the door. As you shed the layers previously protecting the tender flesh from the cold of the outside world, your skin puckers in delight, refreshed by the caress of warmth in the air. Each hair, stands at attention, surveying the dimly lit room for the mystery source. Shiver has abandoned the bones as heat seeps into the core of your body. Smells of warm cinnamon and sweet perfume pull you completely across the threshold and into the arms of the experience.

The earthen walls disappear into the darkness, and the brightness of the flames take center stage, as if this place, in itself, is as boundless as the burning within. They serve only varieties of water here in tall clear glasses that cause the lights to bend into strange, glowing ember-like shadows on the table. You sink into a deep, velvety chair, enchanted by the essence of this haven. In this realm ruled by flame and romance, danger and beauty, you find yourself verging into deep desires and an appetite for liaison with the savory fire.

"Per'aps from the heat, per'aps they are afraid, per'aps they say we crazy 'cause they frosty minds are slow." Her voice comes sweet, like a melody from the adjacent chair. "You new here?" She rises and steps upon the small platform that centers the room. Her long, sleek arms stretch out and in her hands she holds three wicks. Turning slowly towards one of the candles, she dips each one into the kindle, bringing light to life as flame. You feel a flair of intrigue as she gallivants across the stage, as if she, too, has been aroused to the spark of life. She brings the flames close to her naked flesh, revealing her combustible romance and trust of this indefinite lover. Running her hands over and through the untamed, orange glow, she, in barely one stroke, satisfies your libido. Opening her mouth, her luscious auburn locks fall over her shoulders as her head tilts back. The culminations of wonder and amazement as voyeur have long been reached and this ineffable moment brings curiosity and certainty simultaneously. She brings the flame to her lips and pauses to illuminate her face. After only a moment of consideration, she devours the light entirely. Each consecutive wick is extinguished within her temple, embraced by her lips and admired by you.

Nonchalantly, she returns your gaze and saunters slowly back to the chair beside yours. Her Chesire grin pushes the moment over the edge into laughter. You chuckle along with her, somewhat nervous but mostly relieved, realizing you have forgotten to breathe for the last few moments. Warm and enchanted, you consider the reality of this sanctuary. Grabbing your glass, you drink to extinguish your own voracious appetite.

"Yes, I am new here. I don't believe we've met, I'm..." as you turn her direction, the need for formal introduction is startlingly halted by her mysterious absence. Perhaps, she was a potent mirage, a delightful, ethereal welcome mat. Perhaps, this heat has enlivened something long suppressed by the tension of being in the depth of chill for so long. Perhaps, this cabaret is the heaven each of us, individually, define within ourselves.

Mired in the alchemy of the moment, you decide to try your hand with the fire. You reach down to a wick on a table and explore it. Curled on the end, the metal shaft leads to a small, cloth wrapped tip: the harbinger of danger, the source of that illegitimate lover. You, now, turn to kindle the flames, awestruck as a flood of excitement heats your blood. Moving the wick up and down, the flames dance and twirl with a wooing, windy sound. Enchanting. Power and control over this unfettered element bring the desire to completely harness the life of it. With no reluctance, you spread your lips and bring the wick toward your face. One last, loving gaze as the warmth toasts your lips on the way into your mouth. Extinguished and exhilarated, as the flame has found permanent residence within your spirit.

You turn back toward the chairs and see her there, applauding. You, now have that same Chesire grin as you saunter back towards your muse.

Big Screen Movies Can Be Affordable

David Payne
ENGL 1101

◆◆◆

My wife and I are big movie buffs and have seen just about every movie made in the modern era. As a result, we have inherently passed our fanaticism down to our children. We primarily watch a lot of DVD's at home, but our favorite way to experience a movie is going out to the theater to view it on the" big screen." When we make plans to go out to the theater, my daughters look forward to the planned date with eager anticipation. Since there are five of us, however, to do this on a regular basis would be financially demanding. We would like to go to the movies once or twice a month, especially when a "big screen movie" comes out at the theaters. Nevertheless, with a family our size, this would be an extravagant expense, especially with movie prices at the Regal Cinemas. Therefore, we went in search of a less expensive theater. Fortunately, there is a local theater, the Value Cinemas, that offers movies at discounted rates. We enjoy the Regal Cinemas for its newly released movies and sophisticated atmosphere; however, as a large family that loves going to the movie theater often, we are financially appreciative of the Value Cinemas.

When pulling into the massive parking lot at the Regal Cinemas, we can not help but feel excited that we are going to see a "big screen movie," which is usually an action packed adventure movie, but at the same time, we feel annoyed that we have to park a mile away from the entrance. This is a huge theater with hundreds of people watching movies daily. The theater offers the newest released movies with at least twenty-three choices of different movies every day. This is important to those of us who want to see the movie that people are raving about being a "must see" film. On the contrary the Value Cinemas only offers ten different movies that are one to three months past the original release date. Furthermore, the Value Cinemas does not always get every movie that is released although they do have most of the popular movies. In other words, they usually have the "big screen movies" that my family wants to see.

Another part of the movie theater experience that is important is the atmosphere at the theater. The Regal Cinemas theater is just that, regal. Once one gets beyond the entrance, sees the bright lights, colossal advertisements, and then the wall to wall concession counter, there is an extraordinary feeling of excitement. The concessions at Regal Cinemas add to the atmosphere, offering a large service counter with four to five registers and a staff of eight or nine people working to get one's order as quickly as possible. Moreover, the choice of food is overwhelming, including hotdogs, nachos, popcorn, pretzels, and a wide variety of drinks and candy. The Value Cinemas, on the other hand, has no grand brightly lit entrance and usually only one ticket taker. To the right of the ticket taker is a small concession area that has two registers with three or four people. Despite there being less people at the Value Cinemas, the time it takes to get one's order is ultimately about the same. Furthermore, though the prices of the concessions at both theaters are similar, the Value Cinemas offers free refills on the large drink and popcorn, and this is a good thing.

Along with the smell of the popcorn and the thrill of drinking a large coke, which one experiences at both theaters, there is also an eagerness that comes after all the concessions are bought. It is a sense of urgency to get to the seats we want. Seating at Regal Cinemas is stadium style seating that puts the rows of seats at a steeper incline so that no one's view is impeded. This also enhances the atmosphere of the theater. No one likes to pay to watch a movie and not be able to see because the person in front is too tall to see over. I do not have this problem, however, my wife and children experience this dilemma frequently at the Value Cinemas since it does not have stadium style seating.

Additionally, the atmosphere at both theaters is affected greatly by the price of the tickets. Ticket prices at Regal Cinemas are $10.50 for adult tickets and $8.50 for a child's ticket for a non-matinee movie, which is extremely high.   This means for a large family, the total cost to see a great or not so great movie would be around $47 without concessions and at least $20 more with concessions. Since this price is so high, it most likely deters lower income customers such as teenagers, college students, and perhaps even larger families with children. The Value Cinemas ticket price is only $2 rather than $10.50. This lower price attracts a variety of patrons, particularly teenagers and families with children. Consequently, the occurrence of people talking or babies crying as well as the ever interrupting cell phones can be a distraction more frequently than at Regal Cinemas.

The sophisticated atmosphere at the Regal Cinemas is agreeable, but unless it is just my wife and me or a special movie event, we will experience our movies at Value Cinemas. Furthermore, it is exciting to see a "big screen movie" when it is newly released, except we have found that the screens are big at both theaters. Though the atmosphere is different, the experience is just more affordable and can be enjoyed more often at the Value Cinemas.

***

Why I Like This Essay: The first noticeable strength of this essay is the well-developed introduction. The basic concept, a comparison of two movie theaters, could easily result in an overly simplistic essay; however, the writer provides adequate details to clearly articulate the purpose of, and motivation for, making the comparison. Block format, as opposed to point-by-point format, is the organization pattern for the body of the essay, which is a wise choice as it allows the writer to fully describe the detailed scenes at each location. Development is successful here because of the use of vivid description, especially sensory details; the writer has blended the right amount of narration and description to make this comparison-contrast piece colorful and lively.

Amber Brooks, Instructor of English

On the Other Side

De'Lamoore Downie
ENGL 1101

With a strict mother who delved deeply into Christian teaching, I had no choice but to give in to the tight rules which suffocated me. Her beliefs on how a true Christian child should appear propelled the whip she often struck and the tears which flowed due to shame and being continuously berated. My home experiences as a child has caused me to want to create a less intense, strict environment for my future children. The rules set for me in the past are far stricter than those I would set for my children.

One of the rules set for me in my younger years was that I would have very limited privacy. Telephone conversations were never just between my best friend and me, but a third party was included, my mother. I could never gossip about happenings at a major party or who was dating who because of fear of my mother's disapproval. My bedroom door was required to always be open no matter if I were in the nude. Sneaking make-up on or pretending to do homework were merely dreams never to come true. When I have my children, whether it is a boy or girl, I would easily allow them to have as much privacy as is needed. Their telephone conversations would never be hacked, and I would even provide a lock for their door.

If ever I asked my mother for permission to attend a party or visit the mall with friends, her eyes would open impossibly wide, her stare piercing into my spine. Pretending airplanes were shooting stars, I would wish for just a small taste of freedom, simply to wet my tongue. Mother drove me everywhere. I never saw the inside of another vehicle except on TV or in magazines. In addition, the items in my closet were never those of my choice. I made a pledge that my children should never go through such turmoil. Whenever they want to go shopping, they can freely pick any item of clothing; I will even send them by themselves. Permission will, most times, be granted for them to attend parties too, whatever makes them happy.

"Turn off the lights and go to sleep De'Lamoore!" I heard my mother say those words at exactly ten o'clock for sixteen years. Until the day I moved out of my mother's house, I had a bed time. Late night chatting with a close friend never occurred. I inevitably became a morning person. In the mornings, the pounding on my headboard at six o'clock was routine. My nights were miserable and so were my mornings. After the age of thirteen, I will allow my children to go to bed at any time they please, but not in the wee hours of the morning, of course. They say the early bird catches the worm, and in effect, I would require my children to wake up early and make an exception on weekends.

A person, a child especially, should be given the opportunity to express himself or herself freely, whether it is through style of clothing or in a private journal. I believe that when teenagers are allowed to roam freely into the world, to an extent, they are able to make mistakes and hopefully correct them. If they live sheltered lives, void of certain life experiences such as party going or travelling by themselves, how are they to develop common sense and the ability to make certain life choices? An old saying states, "Experience teaches wisdom." Because of this, my children will not live the sheltered, protected life I did. I want them to become men of wisdom.

Managing Our Inheritance

Crystal Shahid
ENGL 1101

◆◆◆

We shared the proud inheritance of American Muslim, and our latest crime scene was a Road Race. As hundreds of women covered in scarves and burka (a dress of Muslim women who only shows their eyes) ran through the otherwise quiet neighborhoods of middle class East Atlanta, my fellow runners and I witnessed two white women take off running and screaming in the opposite direction as if a bomb had just exploded in front of them. On that day, my Muslim sisters and I had been unofficially convicted of the crime of being Muslim by two white women who thought that five hundred Muslims running through the streets suggested some kind of terroristic rebellion. I never spoke up about that crime scene in East Atlanta, but in the essay "Black Men and Public Space," author Brent Staples bravely expresses a range of emotions about his unwieldy inheritance as a Black man. Staples effectively uses imagery and language to express his ambivalence of alienation and acceptance about his ability to alter public spaces in ugly ways. While I will never truly know what it is like to be a Black man in public spaces, I can certainly empathize with the mixed emotions of an inheritance that I cannot change.

To convey his sense of alienation, Staples uses imagery in many of the scenes he describes. He is a black man, broad, six feet two inches with a beard and billowing hair, and he is well aware of his ability to alter public space in ways that make people uncomfortable and fearful of his capabilities. "Ever the suspect, a fearsome entity with whom pedestrians avoid making eye contact" (Staples 612) impresses upon me that Staples is suspicious and should therefore be avoided at all costs. In other scenes, I imagine Staples hiding in crevices as a young boy "scarcely noticeable," and I even sense his loneliness as he peruses a jewelry store without a companion. He describes himself as "an avid nightwalker" on the streets of New York, and references the distance between himself and another walker as "a vast unnerving gulf" (611). He was always the object of some unpleasant situation with not only the police, but doormen, business owners, cabdrivers, and even pedestrians who perceived him as a potentially violent threat. The images of his night walks alone on deserted streets, the nervous door-locking of drivers as he crossed the street in front of them, standing on the train platform by himself, and his shadowy existence as a young boy all infer Staples's sense of isolation and disassociation.

Although the imagery in his essay denotes alienation, Staples also uses language to express his contrasting feeling of acceptance. "I understand, of course, that the danger they perceive is not a hallucination" is an example of how Staples accepts that women's perceptions of Black men are not unjustified (611). In accepting his unwieldy inheritance, Staples admits to the truth about young black males being "drastically overrepresented among the perpetrators of [street] violence" (611). In fact, he has developed strategies that suggest he acknowledges his own intimidation factors and is willing to counter those factors with pleasantries and good will when he says, "I now take precautions to make myself less threatening. I move about with care, particularly late in the evening" (611-612). Staples assumes the burden of guilt of his unwieldy

inheritance, but instead of expressing bitterness, he discovers
ways of making others feel more at ease. To reduce the tension
between himself and potential "victims" of fear, on his night
walks alone, Staples whistles classical tunes from "Beethoven
and Vivaldi and the more classical composers" that make him
seem harmless, and he is ever careful to be "calm and extremely
congenial" during his interaction with police (612). Staples's
language confirms that he accepts the reasoning behind his
alienation, but challenges others to accept the olive branches he
extends in peace.

Whether we are men, women, black, white, Christian,
Muslim, King, or peasant, we have all inherited something that is
beyond our control. Feeling mixed emotions about an
"inheritance" that we cannot change connects us in an unspoken
brotherhood. Without the brave tone of Brent Staples's essay, I
would have never known that I, a young Muslim woman, have
an emotional connection to a Black journalist from Chester,
Pennsylvania. No matter the means of expression we choose to
convey our mixed emotions about our inheritances, we should
remember one thing that although some of our inheritances can
be unwieldy, intimidating, or fearful to others, there are still
peaceful measures we can take to make those inheritances less
threatening and simultaneously keep ourselves from feeling
alienated and isolated.

Works Cited

Staples, Brent. "Black Men and Public Space." *Steps to Writing Well*, Ed. Jean Wyrick. 8th ed. Boston: Wadsworth, 2011. 611-613. Print.

Easier Said Than Done: The Contradictions of Christopher McCandless and their Interpretation by Jon Krakauer

Walker Kirkland
ENGL 1101H

♦♦♦

Chris McCandless is a man portrayed as an independent, idealistic adventurer – a spiritual explorer out to discover the world – in Jon Krakauer's book *Into the Wild*, yet who was McCandless in reality? He could also be described as impulsive, inconsistent, reliant on the good grace of others, and incapable of conquering challenges to his goals. While there is no longer a way to get to know the true Chris McCandless, the contradictions between his ideals and his actions can be understood through his journals, the books he carried, the impressions he left behind, and through the author's interpretation. Taken together, these sources leave one to wonder if Krakauer's interpretation of his hero's actions gives sufficient weight to the discrepancies between the McCandless he writes about and the McCandless evidenced in those records left behind. In the same way that McCandless so often turns away from the obstacles in his life, Krakauer turns away from the obstacle of fully analyzing the impact McCandless's flights have upon himself and others.

Many times within *Into the Wild*, McCandless denies his reliance on money. When he visits the Detrital Wash, McCandless documents himself burning paper money (Krakauer 29). When Jan Burres finds him scavenging edible plants, McCandless tells her he has no need for money (30). This stance is often contradicted, however. Every time McCandless comes to a new city, he buries what cash and valuables he has outside city limits for safekeeping, then looks for work; at the same time, he is not volunteering at shelters to feed the hungry. He is working for money. Before each adventure, McCandless saves cash to buy supplies. Oddly though, it seems that he goes through a cycle of saving money, going on a trip where he either spends or destroys that money, then earns new money. It is unclear whether he feels that ridding himself of cash is freeing, but what is clear is Chris McCandless's consistent reliance on monetary currency.

In a letter to his sister, McCandless passionately expresses his fondness for his 1982 Datsun, stating that it is "... a car that has in all those thousands of miles not given me a single problem, a car that I will never trade in, a car that I am very strongly attached to ..." (21). Even though he loves this car, he abandons it the first time he has any trouble with it. The car's problem is a result of McCandless's lack of planning; he parks in an area that carries water runoff during flash flooding. Instead of taking responsibility for his choices, he writes: "This piece of shit has been abandoned. Whoever can get it out of here can have it" (26). Not only does he leave his car, but he also leaves most of his belongings in it, including twenty-five pounds of rice and his fishing pole. He is such an adamant defender of his yellow Datsun that McCandless's father finds it "mind-boggling" to learn Chris had abandoned the car (32). This is just one example in a pattern of behavior that McCandless exhibits during his travels. Whenever he faces an obstacle to his plans, he becomes frustrated and abandons them for an easier alternative. This trait contrasts with the idea of the unencumbered, natural explorer that Krakauer attempts to portray, and it instead points to McCandless's immaturity, or at least his inability to confront his problems rather than turning away from them.

He bases his faith in his ability to survive in the wilds of Alaska on his thirty-six days of experience subsisting on rice and caught fish on the Gulf of California (162). In addition, he has long experience living off as little food as possible while tramping around the country foraging plants. However, many of the people he befriended noted how ravenously he ate when in their company, and often at their expense. When he is on an adventure, he can live off very little, but as soon as he comes back to society, he takes advantage of the benefits it affords to some degree. "'I had Alex over to the house for supper just about every night,' Borah continues. 'He was a big eater. Never left any food on his plate. Never'" (qtd. in Krakauer 63). There is always that safety net of readily available food and friendship whenever McCandless needs it until he becomes trapped in Alaska. At least in the beginning, he goes through a period during which he has difficulty catching game. Things improve somewhat as time goes on, but for the most part, he is killing small, lean animals that offer little in the way of caloric intake – especially when contrasted to the amount of energy McCandless expends to hunt, dress, and cook these creatures (188).

Regardless of whether or not McCandless experiences any kind of poisoning from legumes, it is likely that once he is trapped on the west side of the Teklanika River, he is in constant danger of dying from starvation. Krakauer already describes the ill-fated adventurer as looking "alarmingly gaunt" in a self portrait taken the day of his intended departure (169). Once he is cut off, McCandless slowly deteriorates. He has no option of coming back to his friends for a free meal. As he weakens and is forced to rely solely on plants for sustenance, McCandless's predicament becomes more and more regrettable. He is alone in the wild for nearly three times as long as his trip to the coast of Mexico. The ability to subsist on rice, game, and other plant life was never a permanent solution given his level of expertise. He may never have anticipated such an extended stay, or fully realized his need for access to food, but his failure to make any plan for such an eventuality is one more example of his tendency to turn away from problems rather than address them.

McCandless wants to explore the wild like adventurers in times gone by before there were maps to guide the way (174).

He takes off on adventures without plotting a course, only planning a final destination. This is exemplified by his canoe trip down the Colorado River. He just hops in his craft and heads south, hoping to reach the Gulf of California. He does not conduct detailed research ahead of time to find out if there are any known impediments to, or special needs for, the journey. As a result, he ends up lost, frustrated, and desperate for help. Luckily for McCandless, he finds a pair of Mexican canal officials who have come prepared with a map. Upon becoming lost again, McCandless is rescued by some hunters who tow him to his final destination (32-35). During most of his adventures, when an unprepared McCandless runs into trouble, he relies on the assistance of those who *have* prepared themselves. Even if another explorer had the desire to simulate an expedition into a completely unknown landscape, it is highly likely he or she would embark on such a course with a depth of knowledge and experience that McCandless did not seek to attain. He could have practiced scouting out rivers or learned canoeing techniques for such a journey from an expert. However, as Krakauer writes, "He tried to live entirely off the country – and he tried to do it without bothering to master beforehand the full repertoire of crucial skills" (181-182). Chris McCandless goes on his impulsive excursions carrying only his ideals and what little experience he picks up along the way.

Krakauer draws parallels between McCandless and a number of other figures in history in order to give the reader some perspective on his protagonist's state of mind and his outcome. The contrast between McCandless's actions and the actions of the Mayor of Hippie Cove is of particular interest. Rather than seeking to enter the wild for a short period of time and live without modern material conveniences, Gene Rosellini ("the Mayor") sought to live in the wild for as long as it took to complete his experiment of regressing to the lifestyle of primitive man. He used no tools, weapons, or shelters provided by modern society. Instead, he lived off the land using stone tools and handmade weapons (73-75). Rosellini was successful at this practice for decades. McCandless, however, carries modern tools and weapons and uses the shelter provided by the bus. He professes to be against modern excesses, shedding many of them, but he does not fully take advantage of methods that have been used by his human ancestors in millennia gone by. Unlike Rosellini, McCandless only partly splits from American culture and convenience. His journeys are a brief excursion into the realm of nature, divided by his inevitable return to the society for which he expresses such distaste.

When McCandless is ready to leave the wild, he encounters the difficult obstacle of the Teklanika River. Besides the fact that he turns around and goes back to the bus, the only true evidence readers have of McCandless's state of mind at that moment is his journal entry: "Disaster. ... Rained in. River look impossible. Lonely, scared" (170). From this, Krakauer derives an explanation of McCandless "weighing his options" and deciding upon "the most prudent course," to return to the shelter of the bus and wait out the summer (171). There is no indication of McCandless making any effort to scout up and down the river to find a more suitable crossing point. The gauging station is only half a mile away from the remnant of the Stampede Trail on which he treads. He has no United States Geological Survey map, but he could have been able to see the aluminum basket hanging suspended on the steel cable spanning the river (173). There is no evidence that he attempts to find an area of the river with shallower waters or an area farther away from the rapids. It is, therefore, just as reasonable, if not more so, to assume that McCandless abandons his plans once again when he faces an obstacle to his goals. He returns to the civilized safety of the bus, his haven from the wild.

As an author for *Outside* magazine, a mountain climber, an adventurer, and as a man who had issues with his father during adolescence, Jon Krakauer seems to have much in common with Chris McCandless. Krakauer clearly identifies with his protagonist through most of the book and seems to respect his moral convictions and go-it-alone attitude. He draws parallels between their backgrounds and life choices and even compares his own Alaskan adventures with those of McCandless. This identification with McCandless leads the author to write about him in a fairly positive light while still maintaining a respectable amount of objectivity for the reader. Krakauer does not allow his opinion of McCandless to stop him from writing about his inconsistencies, and he does not let it stop him from writing about the pain which McCandless's actions cause his family and friends.

It seems, however, that Krakauer's kinship to McCandless causes him to deemphasize the pain that McCandless's actions cause those who love him, possibly because of Krakauer's interest in preserving the privacy of McCandless's family members. McCandless's apparent self-absorption causes his parents and his siblings agonizing stress, grief, and emotional pain from the time he abandons them after his college graduation. During this period, his mother, for example, always leaves a note for her son when she goes out, regularly inspects hitchhikers for her son's likeness, and hears his voice in her dreams (125-126). His inability to maintain an intimate relationship with his family members or with anyone he meets is as important a part of his personal motivation as is his desire to commune with nature. Krakauer does not completely gloss over this aspect of the story, but he does refuse to speculate as to the reasons behind McCandless's interpersonal behavior – much more so than he declines to speculate on the romance of the wanderer's self-reliance and independent spirit. Krakauer dismisses attempts by others to explain McCandless's behavior from a psychological standpoint, stating, "this sort of posthumous off-the-rack psychoanalysis is a dubious, highly speculative enterprise that inevitably demeans and trivializes the absent analysand" (184). However, just five pages later, the author himself is posthumously analyzing McCandless, interpreting his statement "HAPPINESS ONLY REAL WHEN SHARED" to mean the young man has changed his outlook on life, given up his traveling lifestyle, and wants to form relationships and join society (189).

Furthermore, glorification and idolization of Chris McCandless's actions very likely will inspire certain readers to mimic the deceased man. Repeatedly pointing out the strengths of McCandless's character creates an image of his life that misrepresents the true impact of his choices as well as the affect it had on others. In the "Author's Note" Krakauer states, "one or two seemingly insignificant blunders" are all that cost McCandless his life, even going so far as to call these "innocent mistakes." Rather than focusing on the fact that McCandless's reckless choices and lack of planning are the reasons he dies, Krakauer chooses to infer that the young man is free of any blame. Inspiring a new generation to explore their world, to develop their own philosophies of life, is an outcome that is hard to criticize. However, impressing the idea that McCandless's choices are worthy of unexamined admiration, or even emulation, has the potential of doing harm to even more lives.

Through both his actions and words, Chris McCandless can certainly be viewed as an idealistic person. However, his lofty ideals often stretch the limit of what is possible. As a result, his own actions frequently contradict the ideals he professes to hold dear: his reliance on money despite his opposition to it, his reliance on friends for the nourishment he does not provide himself, and his continued refusal to prepare for the dangers of the wild despite his reverence for its other qualities. Most prominent, though, is McCandless's tendency to alter his goals rather than confront his problems. This personality trait leads to heartbreak for his family and has significant impact on the path he takes in life. Ultimately, it is a factor in the decisions that result in his death. *Into the Wild* does a good job helping readers identify with McCandless throughout, but in the end, Krakauer fails to emphasize the attributes of Chris McCandless's personality that contribute greatly to the predicament in which he finds himself at the end of his life.

Works Cited

Krakauer, Jon. *Into the Wild*. New York: Anchor, 1997. Print.

Alcohol in a Glass

Elizabeth Morris
ENGL 1102

Most people will never have to endure the hardship of having an alcoholic as a parent. Those same people will never understand the strain that is put on the offspring of an alcoholic; the brutal chore of having to look after the younger, weaker siblings, and being forced to grow up too fast. Most people do not understand how the simple tainted beverage of alcohol has a major impact on the lives of every member in a family. People who live without this struggle are lucky. For centuries, the infectious drink has been misused and abused by those who wish to drown out their suffering and sorrows while they desperately search for relief from everyday life. While in search of peace and solace, alcoholics continue to destroy the best part of themselves until there is only malice left. In the play, *The Glass Menagerie,* Tennessee Williams expresses the pressures which Tom Wingfield feels within his home life and subtly alludes to the cause of Tom and his father's pitiful addiction. Throughout the play, Williams uses his characters to portray not only the negative effects of alcohol, but also to show how an alcoholic parent can ruin a family.

From the very beginning of the play, the audience admires Tom, the youngest member of the household, who seems to be dealing with the weight of not only his nagging mother pressing heavily over his shoulders, but also his absent father, whom he must now take the place of. These two reoccurring stressors constantly inhabit Tom's mind as he suffers through his day to day life working as a lowly warehouse worker. When he comes home at night, Tom often becomes annoyed by Amanda's barrage of nagging comments:

> I think you've been doing things that you're ashamed of. That's why you act like this. I don't believe that you go every night to the movies. Nobody goes to the movies night after night.

Nobody in their right minds goes to the movies as often as you pretend to. People don't go to the movies at nearly midnight, and movies don't let out at two A.M. Come in stumbling. Muttering to yourself like a maniac! You get three hours' sleep and then go to work. Oh, I can picture the way you're doing down there. Moping, doping, because you're in no condition. (3.31, Amanda).

In this scene, Amanda is pointing out all the flaws in Tom's lifestyle which she is not pleased with, cutting him down for him trying to live his own life outside of his home, and trying to find adventure beyond his current status. Amanda is combining her fears of Tom's negative behavior into her solitary fear that her son will turn into a man who drinks, just like the man she unfortunately married. However, her fears only push Tom farther away from the family and closer to following in his father's footsteps. For example, after the heated argument with his mother, Tom accidently breaks Laura's most valuable possession, her glass menagerie, by throwing his jacket in an angry attempt to leave. Although Tom shows genuine concern for Laura's suffering, he still allows his father's habits to become his own. Tom storms out of the apartment, heads toward the movies, and buries his woes in a bottle while he relentlessly seeks adventure. He stays at the movies all night and returns home in a drunken stupor, "Tom fishes in his pockets for his door key, removing a motley assortment of articles in the search, including a perfect shower of movie ticket stubs and an empty bottle" (Scene Four, stage directions). With this bit of information, Williams is informing his audience that Tom was, in fact, telling the truth about going to the movies, as well as hinting that Tom is indeed becoming more like his drunkard father. This scene not only foreshadows the adventure that he will eventually embark on his own just as his father did, but also the burden that his suffering mother must bear.

Amanda's fears over her children's future blind her from the truth of Tom's intentions. In the middle of the play, Amanda confronts Tom of her worries about him turning into a drinking man like his father, "Promise, son, you'll- never be a drunkard!" (4.41, Amanda). It can be noted that Amanda is ignoring the present problems of Tom's going to the movies late at night, which was once her main concern, and instead is putting all her focus on his drinking. Amanda is making the assumption that drinking is a symbol for all undesirable activities in Tom's life. She worries that soon Tom will turn into the type of man his father was. The illuminating words that provide the most evidence for Tom's father being a drunkard can be noted when Amanda tells Tom, "Old maids are better off than wives of drunkards!" (5.77, Amanda). Amanda associates alcoholism with her husband and, therefore, with irresponsibility and abandonment. She resents that she married a man who drank and then left without reason. Amanda's main concern is that Tom will escalade from drinking, become more irresponsible, and ultimately leave the women to care for themselves, just as his father did before him. Her constant worries over her children misguide her judgment, turning Amanda into a harping, over protective mother who is unable to allow her children to live their own life. Thus, the Wingfield family is left to crumble under the weight of an over bearing mother and an absent drunkard father.

Having an alcoholic parent is difficult for any family to deal with. From break downs to abuse and neglect, alcohol destroys the lives of everyone it touches. In the play *The Glass Menagerie,* Williams is trying to convey the idea that parents who drink have a negative impact on not only their spouses, but also their children. The Wingfield family knew too well the suffering which emanated from the tainted drink. Amanda is a woman caught in the deep sinking web of drinking men. Of all the wondrous suitors she spoke of, she chose to marry a charming man who worked for the telephone company. Her husband, a long distance lover, turned into a drunkard, and then vanished from sight makes Amanda desolate and overbearing toward her children. Her internal resentment forced Tom to become the man she had grown to despise. Through his characters, Williams is pointing out the flaws of a family torn apart by an alcoholic father. He intends to enlighten the audience of how easily a home can be destroyed by the vile drink and those who consume it as his own family experienced. Growing up, Williams and his father did not see eye to eye. As Michael

Flachmann points out when mentioning Williams' home life, "Tom endured a difficult relationship with his father, Cornelius, because he was domineering, womanizing, and an abusive drunkard" (Flachmann). Williams' mental scars can be found within the play through Tom's character. Tom Wingfield was abandoned by his father and left with the weight of a family on his shoulders. His unfulfilling life as a lowly warehouse worker and the pressures of his harping mother compels Tom to dissolve his hostility by drinking. He feels his only way out is in the bottom of a bottle because that is the only remedy to his heart's sufferin. However, in the end, Tom realizes that he is much stronger, and much wiser than his father. Tom frees himself of the burdens which he carries with his mother's apartment and allows himself to become something better in the world so that he can later come back to care for his family the proper way; something his father never did. Tom made the decision to leave his family, but this sacrifice allowed him to find himself sober. In the final lines of the play, Williams allows his audience to see that even with the worst setbacks, children of drunken parents can set themselves free.

***

Why I Like This Essay: I liked this essay because the writer had an original idea about the play's theme. Because her reading of the play was quite different from that of most of her classmates, she used her evidence to carefully construct a persuasive argument. She used the primary text effectively to convince me of her argument, and she was also able to find a secondary source to add additional support to her argument.
Katherine Perry, Assistant Professor of English

Works Cited

Flachmann, Michael. *An Introduction to The Glass Menagerie.*
   Camp Shakespeare, 2011. Web. 7 Mar. 2011.
Williams, Tennessee. *The Glass Menagerie.* Chicago: Penguin,
   1944. Print.

Chekhov's Last Play: The Cherry Orchard as Comedy

Tuan Minh Khong
ENGL 1102

◆◆◆

Anton Chekhov is a well-known Russian writer who dedicated his whole life to literature and perfecting his craft. He wrote many short stories and plays pertaining to the human experience. Although his short stories received great praises, many of his plays did not. The reason is that critics often misunderstand "the nature of his comedies" (Latham 21). *The Cherry Orchard*, a play about "the impoverishment of an aristocratic family," is a comedy, Chekhov insisted (Latham 22). Many analysts see it as more of a drama. "Even Stanislavsky, the founder of the Moscow Art Theatre," misinterprets Chekhov's intention and stages "the premier of the play as a somber tragedy" (Brand 1). However, the play borderlines what is a "tragedy" and a "farce" (Latham 22). It is this peculiar point that Chekhov wants to illustrate and explore. As he puts it plainly, "I will describe life to you truthfully, that is artistically and you will see in it what you have not seen before, what you never noticed before: its divergence from the norms, its contradictions" (qtd. in

Magarshack 32). *The Cherry Orchard* is a unique comedy due to Chekhov's effective application of comedic elements.

Through the use of abnormal characters, Chekhov pokes fun at the aristocratic family's inability to cope with changes when faced with a dilemma. For example, Madame Ranevsky (Lyubov Andreyevna), the owner of an estate on the verge of bankruptcy, is a "creature of moods" (Latham 23). "Mrs. Ranevsky interacts with everyone in mercurial oscillations between tears and laughter" (Tait 89). Although described by Lopahin, a former peasant, as a "good-natured," "kind-hearted," and "splendid" woman, her interactions with other characters, say otherwise. She addresses Firs as "old man" (Chekhov 62), disregards what he has to say, and openly comments on how funny looking Trofimov is (Chekhov 66). Additionally, "she cannot reconcile herself to giving up her past, her innocent youth, and her formerly carefree life" ("Cherry Orchard" 1). She is fond of her old nursery. Looking out the window from the room, she daydreams about a joyful time in her past when she was a child playing in the cherry orchard (Chekhov 66). As an adult, "she cannot assume the financial and emotional responsibility demanded of her" ("Cherry Orchard" 1). She is indecisive in deriving a plan to save her estate and the cherry orchard. Although heavily in debt, Madame Ranevsky spends money lavishly whenever she goes out. While at home, her servants struggle for food (Chekhov 76). In Act III, her thoughtless expenditure continues when she hosts a party accompanied by a Jewish orchestra. In the meantime, the estate is auctioned and all is lost. "Madame Ranevsky is irresponsible, negligent, and self-destructive. Her indolence and uncontrollable extravagance bring her house tumbling down" ("Cherry Orchard"). As head of the household, she is an incompetent leader who is unable to make smart decisions on her own, and is unwilling to grasp the magnitude of her crisis. She is like a child, as depicted by her constant mood swings and foolish actions. Madame Ranevsky's innocence is what makes her a comic figure because she can only dwell in her past. Therefore, she is incapable of functioning as an adult in the real world.

Gaev (Leonid Andreyevitch), like his sister Madame Ranevsky, is an abnormal character. At fifty-one, "Gaev treats life no more serious than the game of billards which he plays in his imaginations…Gaev's ridiculousness is accentuated by his continual eating of candies" (Latham 23). He claims to have eaten up his fortune in "caramels" (Chekhov 73). "This candy eating is a symbol of his childishness and of his unfitness for the adult world. Even Firs, the butler, treats him like a child, worrying whether he is dressed properly when he goes out and bringing him his coat when it is cold" (Latham 23). Furthermore, Gaev contradicts himself when he made a promise that he cannot possibly keep. He has sworn upon his soul to save the properties, but when it comes time to carry out with the plan, he is nowhere to be found (Chekhov 68). Unlike Madame Ranevsky, however, Gaev actually takes the initiative to help with their problems even though his ideas are so farfetched.

Another abnormal character is Lopakhin (Yermolay Alexeyevitch), a successful businessman who is "caught in his childhood sense of inferiority" (Latham 24). His father and grandfather, who are serfs, both worked for the Ranevskys. Because of his humble beginning, Lopakhin is constantly haunted by his former social status. For example, when he sees that Dunyasha, a maid, is "dressed like a lady" with her hair "done up," he tells her: "One must know one's place" (Chekhov 57). He says to Dunyasha that he is a rich man now, but for all his money, he is still a peasant (Chekhov 57-58). Throughout most of the play, Lopakhin appears be overly concerned with Madame Ranevsky's situation and makes attempts to help save her properties, when in reality, he is only plotting his scheme to overtake the oppressive aristocratic family. Lopakhin suggests that the cherry orchard should be "cut up into building plots, and then let on lease for summer villas" (Chekhov 63). Madame Ranevsky's indecisiveness leads to the discovery behind Lopakhin true motive. He merely sees the cherry orchard as an excellent site for development (Magarshack 170). In Act III, to everyone's surprise, Lopakhin reveals himself as a new master, the owner of the estate and the cherry orchard. He plans on chopping down all the trees, which Madame Ranevsky is so fond of, to make space for building houses (Chekhov 86). No longer is he a "low-born Knave, " as Gaev often refers to him (Chekhov 65). In the end, Lopakhin chooses personal wealth over the kindness that Madame Ranevsky has shown him when he was still a peasant. He exposes signs of arrogance when he excessively celebrates his new purchases and immediately makes demands on doing things to his liking. It is comical and tragic because Lopakhin, who is perceived as the chief savior, a hero in the catastrophe, betrays everyone's trust for his own advancement in life.

Chekhov uses farcical incidents to heighten *The Cherry Orchard* as a comedy. For instance, the audience finds Epihodov's arrival on the scene in Act I hilarious. The squeaking floor boards reinforce the cumbersome entry of Epihodov as he also wears a pair of new boots that "creak." He enters the setting with some inappropriate flowers for Dunyasha to put in the dining room. While trying to manage a hat and shake Dunyasha's hand at the same time, he drops the flowers to the floor. As he leaves the room, he stumbles against a chair which falls over (Chekhov 58). In Act II, the audience is exposed to Epihodov's insanity when he shows everyone the revolver that he carries with him around should he decide to shoot himself (Chekhov 70). His clumsiness is only appropriate for the name in which he is given by others. Because he is accident-prone, "they call him two and twenty misfortunes" (Chekhov 58). He himself claims that he is tossed around by fate. "Every day some misfortune befalls me. I don't complain. I'm used to it, and I wear a smiling face" (Chekhov 58).

Another broad comic figure is the character of Trofimov (Pyotr Sergeyevitch). It is satirical to regard him as the only "idealist" in the play, but this is exactly the author's intention (Brand 2). Chekhov wants to show Trofimov as "slothful, superficial, fatuous, and undersexed" (Brand 2). "Trofimov's exterior itself is comic," which leads to many awkward incidents (Magarshack 178). For example, in Act I when he goes to meet Madame Ranevsky, at first she does not recognize who he is. She "half cries and half laughs when she looks at his beard" (178). She is depressed at how he looks and questions why he has grown so "old" and "ugly." (Chekhov 66). Trofimov replies sarcastically as if he is proud of the way he looks. He says: "A peasant-woman in the train called me a mangy-looking gentleman" (66). Madame Ranevsky then comments on what a "pretty little student" he used to be, but now he looks hideous (66). She finds it hard to believe that he is still a student. He concurs: "I seem likely to be a perpetual student" (66). Trofimov is a "perpetual student" in more senses than one. "He is the eternal adolescent because reason means everything to him and experience nothing. He belongs to those men who never really grow up because they can never see the distinction between what is reasonable and what is wise. Trofimov sees through everybody except himself" (Magarshack 178). In Act III, he tells Madame Ranevsky: "for once in your life you must face the truth!" (Chekhov 81). When it comes to himself, "all he does is to utter cliché" (Magarshack 178). When Madame Ranevsky calls him a virgin and a freak, Trofimov is so infuriated that he utters this cliché : "All is over between us!" (Magarshack 178). As he rushes out of the room he falls and crashes down the stairs, thus intensifying the humor.

Other farcical incidents are abundant throughout the play. For instance, Firs's mumbles, dogs barking, and a drunken peasant's foul language are background noises or distractions behind the conversations of the main characters. The audience also finds Gaev's speech to a book case rather humorous.

> Yes... It is a thing... (feeling the bookcase). Dear, honoured bookcase! Hail to thee who for more than a hundred years hast served the pure ideals of good and justice; thy silent call to fruitful labour has never flagged in those hundred years, maintaining (in tears) in the generations of man, courage and faith in a brighter future and fostering in us ideals of good and social consciousness (a pause) (Chekhov 64).

Only after a "mawkish moment of self-awareness", does Gaev realize how ludicrous his speech was (Latham 24). Madame Ranevsky makes a similar senseless act when she kisses and embraces the bookcase, telling it how happy she is in the moment (Chekhov 62).

Chekov incorporates comical themes in *The Cherry Orchard* to glorify it as a comedy. He softens serious matters in society by ridiculing the theme of the "passing of an old order" and unrequited love (Latham 22). For instance, Firs, the old manservant, laments the future and glorifies the past, a time where servants know their places. He does not agree with the emancipation and stays in service even after being freed (Chekhov 74). Despite his loyalty to serve, he is tragically forgotten and left for death at the end of the play. Just like Firs, Madame Ranevsky and her brother are reluctant to see the passing of the old order. They tend to retreat to the time when everything is certain, and refuse to confront the impending sale of their properties by ignoring the matter until it is too late.

All social classes are subjected to Chekhov's mockery. In the play, the theme of unrequited love is made ludicrous as shown by the love triangle between the servants: Epihodov, Dunyasha, and Yasha. Epihodov who is madly in love with Dunyasha, proposes to her and desperately tries to win her heart. His "awkwardness upsets Dunyasha's ideal of a romantic hero" (Tait 94). She is hesitant to accept his proposal because she thinks that he is less educated than Yasha, whom she has fallen in love with. Dunyasha throws herself at Yasha without inhibition, but he does not return her affection. He is simply playing with her heart. At one time in the play, he kisses her, then asks her to leave for it would look bad for them to be seen together (Chekhov 71). Both Epihodov and Yasha believe that they are superior to Dunyasha. On the other hand, Dunyasha thinks and behaves as if she is a classy lady, not a servant. Because the characters think so highly of themselves they are incapable of establishing a committed relationship for fear of being matched up with a subordinate partner.

The relationship between Lopakhin and Varya, Madame Ranevsky's adopted daughter, is a strange one. Lopahin expresses some interest in Varya, but he does not propose to her (Valency 94). At various points in the play, Madame Ranevsky, Gaev, and Tromfimov suggest that the couple should get married. Lopakhin, who adores Madame Ranevsky, says he cannot propose to Varya without her there. "It is clear that she is the secret love of his life, his ideal of womanhood and perhaps the true reason why he will not compromise by marrying Varya (Valency 94). Although Lopakhin thrives in the business world, he is unsuccessful in his personal life. In secretly loving Madame

Ranevsky, he forfeits his chance of happiness with a hardworking, caring, and loyal person like Varya.

"A gendering of love and suffering in *The Cherry Orchard* is evident in the convergence of mourning and loss, and femininity and melancholia, in the identity of Mrs. Ranevsky" (Tait 90). First of all, she marries a drunkard who dies from drinking champagne. To her misery, she falls in love with another man and immediately disaster strikes; her son drowns in the river. Showing lack of responsibility, she leaves her daughters behind and escapes with her lover to Mentone where he becomes ill. For three long years, she takes care of him, but he abandons her for another woman. In the end, he begs forgiveness and entreats her to return (Chekhov 73). Ironically, after all the pain and suffering that he has inflicted upon her, she returns to him. While the spectators should show sympathy for Madame Ranevsky's misfortunes and bad romance, they cannot stop laughing at her absurdity because it leaves them puzzled. Why would she return to a man who has been unfaithful, robs her of everything, puts her in debt, and jeopardizes her family's well-being?

The only compatible match in the play is also made fun of. Charlotta Ivanovna, a governess who "soliloquizes about her rootlessness and life's emptiness" (Brand 2), captures Semyonov-Pishtchik's declaration of love (Tait 94). These two are compatible because they are both clownish figures. Charlotta seeks every opportunity to perform her circus acts which she learned at the traveling fairs. She "cannot fix her social self in the world that she confronts, and her interiority is described as a state of emotional flux. By association with her tricks, her expressive acts present an illusionary self" (95). Pishtchik matches Charlotta's ridiculousness by trying to swallow all of Madame Ranevsky's pills, comparing himself to a horse, and begging for money with every chance he gets.

In *The Cherry Orchard*, Chekhov creates the realm of contradictory elements and embeds in this world underlying humor to form a brand of comedy uniquely his own. Although the play has a melancholic overtone which resembles a tragedy, the author has another intention for it. "In his revelation of the ludicrous in human nature Chekhov successfully achieves a very rare blend of sympathetic and judicial comedy" (Latham 29). To accomplish this, he places his characters through the worse of predicaments and shows how they are unfit to deal with the challenges that arise in the material world. Chekhov ridicules his characters regardless of their classes in society. "He did not see the passing of the old order as tragic, and, in emphasizing the social uselessness of the aristocratic family, he treats the subject from a comic viewpoint. He sees in them no love, no sense of responsibility; their deepest emotion is only sentiment" (Latham 22). Through the selective arrangement of comedic elements, Chekhov utilizes his fictional, yet symbolic characters to criticize the dysfunctions in society.

Works Cited

Brand, Gerhard, Moe, Christian H. "The Cherry Orchard."
    Magill's Survey of World Literature, Revised Edition
    (January 2009) 1-2. *Literary Reference Center*. Web.
    4 Apr. 2011.

Chekhov, Anton. *The Cherry Orchard. The Plays of Anton*
    Chekhov. New York: Caxton House, Inc., 1945. 57-
    95. Print.

"*The Cherry Orchard.*" *Cyclopedia of Literary Character*,
    Revised Third Edition (January 1998) 1. *Literary*
    Reference Center. Web. 4 Apr. 2011.

Latham, Jacqueline E. M. "The Cherry Orchard as Comedy."
    Educational Theatre Journal 10.1 (1958): 21-29.
    JSTOR. Web. 4 Apr. 2011.

Magarshack, David. *The Cherry Orchard. Chekhov New*
    Perspective Edited by Rene Nonna D. Welleck.
    Englewood Cliffs: Prentice-Hall, Inc., 1984. 168-182.
    Print.

Tait, Peta. "Performative Acts of Gendered Emotions and Bodies
    in Chekhov's The Cherry Orchard." *Modern Drama.*
    43.1 (2000): 87-96. *Literary Reference Center*. Web. 25
    Mar. 2011.

Valency, Maurice. *The World of The Cherry Orchard. Anton*
    Chekhov/edited and with an introduction by Harold
    Bloom. New York: Chelsea House, 2000. 94. Print.

***

Why I Like This Essay: Tuan began the 1102 research process by sorting through options in the textbook. At a pivotal point, he said, "I want to do something different. How about Chekhov?" This decision launched his essay on *The Cherry Orchard.* While the first draft included good observations from critics, Tuan took the project a step further. To illustrate comedic elements, he added supporting examples from the drama--Madame Ranevsky's lavish spending amidst debt, Gaev's childishness, Lopakhin's maneuvering. After the essay was graded and the course successfully completed, Tuan agreed to one more revision. The outcome of his hard work on multiple drafts is this published essay.

Jean Hakes, Instructor of English

The Saw

Jeremy Stipcak
ENGL 1102

♦♦♦

Robert Frost is one of the most celebrated American poets to date. His poems reflect himself as a person and everything he believes. His poem, "Out, Out", is no exception. He proclaims the realities of life without appearing cynical or overly emotional. His love for the beauty of nature is clearly shown early in the poem with the speaker noticing the incredible sight of mountains in the background. He also shows his deep dislike for complex machinery not only when the horrific action occurs, but also leading up to that point. By the end, he lets the reader learn his opinion on death as well by observing the secondary characters. Robert Frost's personal feelings and beliefs are brightly shown in "Out, Out" which includes disgust for the Industrial Revolution which can be seen as the saw destroys and kills.

Frost is more or less a naturalist. He sees beauty and understanding in nature which is reflected in his work. The beginning of "Out, Out" is a clear example of his respect for nature. Frost makes a point to notice the landscape in the background. The narrator spots "five mountain ranges, one behind the other, under the sunset far into Vermont" (Frost 55). It can be assumed that the horizon is a beautiful spectacle that would grab the attention of even the busiest man. Frost does a very good job in describing nature scenes that the reader can clearly visualize. It is true that Frost loves nature, and the inverse is also true. Frost hated the Industrial Revolution. He viewed complex machinery as cold, calculating and lifeless. Such a statement is ironic considering the personification of the saw. Frost's feelings for the saw are shown as the snarling and rattling interrupts the narrator from the amazing view of the mountains. The saw's destructive intent is elaborated through the middle of the poem.

"Out, Out" is not one of Frost's typical poems. It does not directly uplift nature above all else; however, it condemns the evil and misgivings that the Industrial Revolution began. The saw is, indeed, characterized as evil. Just to have the words, "snarled and rattled", creates imagery of some kind of beast that warns of an imminent attack. The fact that the day was almost at an end and, no incident had occurred, gives the impression that the saw had planned a surprise attack. It was almost as if the saw was just waiting for the right moment, which hints at premeditation of hostility. Frost wrote that the saw seemed to leap toward the boy's hand as if it suddenly pounced on its prey. Upon the knowledge of the severed limb, the boy as well as the surrounding characters, do not even consider the possibility of the loss of life. The boy seems to be only concerned with his hand when he screams "don't let him cut my hand off" (Frost 55). The poem says nothing more about the saw or its noise most likely because the damage is already done. It can be clearly seen that Frost has distrust for technology because "he knew well its limitations and cautioned against a complete embrace of it" (Fagan 407). Robert Frost also had a healthy view of death which is evident at the end of the poem.

Many people fear death in such a way that the joy of living in the moment is taken from them. Robert Frost, on the other hand, accepts death as a natural course of life. Frost's views point out that tragedy happens, but life goes on. As the boy's pulse was fading, the bystanders already knew the end was near. Frost has a gift in unique word selection that he used in this scene. "Little, less, nothing" is how he described the boy's final heartbeats. The next line gets straight to the point when he describes the mood of the secondary characters. The people simply turn to their obligations because they are alive. No matter how sad or shocked they are over the boy's death, they still have their lives to live. After the narrator announced the boy was dead, he said, "there was no more to build on there" (Frost 55). That line is an example of Frost's ability to take a step back and view death without fear or frantic emotion. It seems the only one in the poem that cannot detach from the scene is the narrator. The people are dispersing, and it would seem that the narrator is still hovering over the dead body. Many people could learn from Frost's viewpoint of death, and they might live a happier life because of it. His views and beliefs are portrayed throughout this poem.

It is quite clear exactly what beliefs Frost held. Throughout his life, he respected natural and even mystical things. "Out, Out" is an indirect example of those beliefs, where the natural final destination of life is death. He accepted this reality without fear or regret. The peace and tranquility that he saw in nature is shown through the destructive power of complex machinery, which he despised. Most of his poems celebrate nature in a direct way. This is a special example of the inverse. He celebrates nature in this poem indirectly by condemning man-made industry. The saw obviously holds no love for the beauty of nature as seen in the poem. The poem not only displays a respect for nature, but it gives insight to the human mind through natural occurrences. It is easy to see why Robert Frost is held in high regards as being one of the best poets in America.

Works Cited

Fagan, Deirdre. Robert Frost A Literary Reference to His Life and Work, New York. Facts on File, 2007.
Frost, Robert. "Out, Out" 1916 Ted Wadley, Coursepack.

***

Why I Like This Essay: Mr. Stipcak provides a sensitive and thoughtful interpretation of Frost's poem. The essay is well-written, with clear sentences, fully developed paragraphs, a strong thesis and conclusion. I appreciate the analysis of imagery, pointing out contrasts, even contradictions which develop irony. For a primary-source literary essay, Mr. Stipcak chose his poem and topic well, and he was able to convey his thoughts and feelings to the reader.
Ted Wadley, Associate Professor of English

Take Back the Night: Feminism in Atwood's *The Handmaid Tale*

Genevieve Devereaux Milliken
ENGL 1102H

♦♦♦

In the Western world, women have forgotten what feminist pioneers have done to pave the way for equality. There is a lackadaisical attitude among females because the grueling battles for equality were fought by past generations. When women forget to use their voices, they risk having them taken away again. Modern women do not need to see feminism as anti-male, but it does need to reflect enthusiasm characteristic of past movements. Through the futuristic dystopia[1] *The Handmaid's Tale*[2], Margaret Atwood demonstrates the extreme nature of a patriarchal society, the results when women become compliant, and ways to re-define feminism in the modern world. In her eventual rebellion against the values of the Republic of Gilead, Offred represents women's liberation through self-preservation and sex that is characteristic of the post-feminist movement in the Western World.

For modern women to understand their future, they must understand their past liberation in terms of what happened, why it happened, and prevent it from happening again. Beginning in the late nineteenth century, women reached for more control over their lives and less control from their fathers, husbands, and society. It is hard to imagine a time when women could not vote, have marriage or property rights, or have meaningful job opportunities, but this is certainly how women lived in the not too distant past. Characteristic to the female consciousness, many women ignored their own injustices and became abolitionists fighting for the elimination of slavery. Lead by mostly white, abolitionist women, The Seneca Falls Convention marked the first time women converged in a central location and organized their grievances, yet women did not receive suffrage until seventy years later.

Expanding on the rights accomplished with the first-wave, the second-wave of feminism lasted from the 1960's to late 1970's. With the 1966 founding of the National Organization for Women (NOW), feminist groups became more aggressive in their tactics by organizing marches plus book, bra, and pornography burnings. At this time, women fervently undertook legal inequalities such as equal pay rights and reproductive rights. This era ended with the internal rift between the anti-pornography feminists and the sexually liberal feminists. Feminists questioned whether pornography was sexually liberating or sadomasochistic. Since the second-wave, feminism has not yet been able to recreate the ardent nature of this movement.

In identifying the historical parallels in *The Handmaid's Tale*, Offred's mother and Moira represent the second- wave of feminism. Offred's mother, who is never named in the book, is a zealous feminist who is unconcerned with gender roles or a traditional nuclear family. Offred remembers her mother's late night book and pornography burnings with contempt because she does not understand their meaning. This misunderstanding is exemplified when Offred's mother says, "As for you, she'd say to me, you're just a backlash. Flash in the pan. History will absolve me" (121). This "backlash" represents a new generation disregarding and degrading the former legal and social gains of second-wave feminism. This disrespect enables a future of confinement, such as the Republic of Gilead.

As for Moira, she is a younger version of Offred's mother. Moira has a sense of independence and nonconformity given that she is a lesbian, wears bizarre clothes, and shuns gender roles. Though Offred's best friend, Moira represents a freedom Offred cannot have. However after the takeover of Gilead, Moira gives Offred the courage to take small steps towards liberation. Through Moira's blunt attitude against the Aunts, Offred steps towards rebellion when she says, "There is something powerful in the whispering of obscenities about those in power. There's something delightful about it, something naughty, secretive, forbidden, and thrilling" (222). Even with powerful women surrounding her, Offred cannot seem to find her own voice because she does not have the characteristics of a second-wave feminist.

However, she is representative of a young woman living in the post-feminist period. The post-feminist period started at the beginning of the 1980's. This time period was a withdrawal from the liberal, second-wave of feminism to more conservative views of femininity. Marie Napierkowski describes the period best when she says that the 1980's international political agendas turned to monetary restraint and conservatism. She also theorizes that the freedoms gained in the 1960's resulted in overspending in the 1970's, thus creating a backlash in the 1980's (124). Besides the shift to political restraint, religious fundamentalism, such as the Moral Majority, had a clutch on American family values especially in the role of women. As in most theological patriarchal societies, men convinced women that the definition of femininity was motherhood, not individualism.

Offred embodies the post-feminist period because she is confused with her role as a woman, wife, and mother. She becomes the protagonist because all young women can see her struggles within themselves. In addressing this parallel and quoting Atwood, Jill Swale states:

> Offred herself represents the present generation of young American women, well-educated, wanting a career, but rather scathing of feminism, valuing romantic love and somewhat traditional in some of her thinking. Atwood deliberately chose such a person as an Everywomen with whom the reader can identify. She said, "The voice is that of an ordinary,

more-or-less cowardly women (rather than a heroine), because I am more interested in social history than in the biography of the outstanding". (37)

Atwood could have gone with a traditional heroine like Louisa May Alcott's Jo March or Kate Chopin's Edna Pontellier, but Offred is triumphant because of her poignant flaws and modern context. Atwood makes Offred suffer the consequences for her acquiescence and disregard of the historical struggles of the first and second feminist movements before she is victorious.

Gilead's[3] social structure is not strictly fictional because it directly depicts aspects of the patriarchal society in the Western World. According to Atwood, the historical parallels between American imperial society and Gilead were relevant when the book was written in 1986 and continue to be so today (Rule 631). Napierkowski explains that Atwood originally tried to set the novel in Canada, but it simply would not fit Canadian culture. Napierkowski illuminates the parallels of the 1980s to Gilead when she says, "The extreme shift toward conservatism in the United States at the time is significant to the social change that created the Republic of Gilead in Atwood's imagination" (124). Atwood, living in Canada then attending college in the United States, had a dual outlook because she could see the hypocrisy of American culture and then experience it for herself.

Atwood places Offred in the Republic in Gilead to show the detrimental effects of a theological and patriarchal society, her enslavement as a Handmaid, then her autonomy. Offred finds her liberation in two ways: self-preservation through her mind and sex through her body. Offred knows that she must survive by being aware of her surroundings at all times. This is illuminated when she says, "Live in the present, make the most of it, it's all you've got" (8) and "I intend to last" (143). Offred's stories of her mother and Moira are devices to preserve herself; however, they serve as warnings as well. Through their stories, Offred becomes cautious and calculated because she realizes that direct rebellion will only lead to death.

In the novel, Offred's mother vanishes when the Gileadean regime begins to take over the United States. Offred does not see her mother again until watching a propaganda video showing women cleaning up toxic waste and sludge. Though it is not mentioned, Offred's mother probably rebels against Gilead given her extreme feminist views or was punished for her participation in feminist organizations. However, Offred is not deterred by her mother's fate; instead it makes her more aware. Her awareness can be seen fully when she says, "I am alive, I breathe, I put my hand out, unfolded, into the sunlight. Where I am is not a prison but a privilege..." (8). Her mother's fate is a warning to Offred not to overtly rebel in Gilead because she will not survive.

Similar to Offred's mother's story, Moira's story serves as mental escape and forewarning to Offred. Moira's[4] defiance leads her to prostitution at the secret men's club, Jezebel's. Offred does not see Moira again until the Commander takes her on their forbidden date. Atwood uses irony to show Moira's fate when she writes, "Moira had power now, she'd been set loose, she'd set herself loose. She was now a loose woman" (133). Moira's fate is a warning that escape is not an option. Instead, Offred must quietly preserve herself by taking calculated risks in remembrance of her mother's and Moira's defiant nature.

Not only does Offred gain self-preservation though her memories of Moira and her mother, she also gains protection by fulfilling her role as a Handmaid. Offred does the shopping and attends "Prayvaganzas", but, most importantly, she uses proper dialogue when talking to Ofglen[5] and Ofwarren. Lucy Freibert believes that the Handmaid's speech etiquette, such as "Blessed be the Fruit" and "Under his Eye," serves to exemplify the biblical element of a handmaid and prevent meaningful conversation (284). Offred also uses the pretense of visiting the Hanging Wall to see if Luke is dead. She utilizes her mind to create her own liberty. Freibert supports this theory when she says, "As she tells her tale, Offred realizes that an embodied imagination, not body alone, offers the real potential for freedom" (287). By putting on a façade she successfully obscures herself from the surveillance of the Eyes and Guardians of Gilead, all while setting herself free in her consciousness.

Offred's most important step to liberation comes from her sexual relationship with the Commander and Nick. In the course of the novel, Offred can be seen progressing from fear, to despair, then boldness (Freibert 286). Her first secret meeting with the Commander exemplifies this boldness which leads to pleasures from her past life. Though it may seem superficial, the lotion and *Vogue* magazines that Offred receives give her hope and a sense of power. However, Freibert notes that Offred eventually realizes "the emptiness of her gains" (288). Adding to her minor luxuries, Offred reads *Hard Times* by Charles Dickens which, surely in Atwood's view, is the most missed indulgence. Also, during one of her visits she gets to use a pen when writing *Nolite te bastardes carborundorum*; this leads her to say, "Pen Is Envy...Just holding it is envy. I envy the Commander [and] his pen" (187). Clearly, this is a reference to Freud's psychological theory of "Penis Envy." Through Offred and the Commander's meetings, Atwood shows that Offred does gain some freedoms, but these freedoms are still subject to a male's discretion.

When Nick first tells Offred to meet the Commander, she thinks that he wants to have forbidden secretive sex. In her essay "'Trust Me': Reading the Romance Plot in Margaret Atwood's *The Handmaid's Tale*, Madonne Miner says that when the Commander pulls out a Scrabble board, Offred realizes that the game *is* the forbidden sexual act (Miner 148). After spelling words like "Larynx" and "Zygote," Offred realizes this sexual nature when she says, "I hold the glossy counters with their smooth edges, finger the letters. The feeling is voluptuous. ...I spell. *Gorge*. What a luxury. The counters are like candies, made of peppermint, cool like that" (139). Atwood makes playing Scrabble the sexual act, rather than copulation, to show the nonsensical restraints of Gilead and Offred's rebellion against them.

Through Nick, Atwood completes Offred's freedom. Offred and Nick's relationship not only lead to sexual freedom but to Offred's escape from Gilead. It is rather peculiar that Atwood chooses a male to free Offred, but Nick resembles a sort of faith in mankind. In her essay, Miner observes that Nick falls into the category of fairy-tale male protagonist, yet his role is important because there is something human in falling in love (164). However, Freibert hypothesizes that it does not matter what his literary role is when she says:

Offred's real breakthrough to her courageous
sexual self comes not with the Commander, who
she soon bores with, but with Nick. …it matters
little whether Nick is the Tempter in the Garden
or the Delivering Angel who arrives in the nick
of time, for he serves to release Offred to sexual
abandonment and freedom to record her tale.
(288)

This sexual freedom can only come when Offred completely
rebels without any restraint or regard for her surrounding of
Gilead. Offred does not know or care if Nick is an Eye, and she
does not know if the "black van" is going to bring her death. It is
Offred's complete leap of faith in Nick that saves her. Through
Nick, Offred is able to escape and tell her tale to everyone
through her tape recordings. These tapes are warnings to every
woman to never take for granted the freedoms feminists have
fought for in the Western World.

The Handmaid's Tale shows it is necessary to have
reverence for feminism because the risk of repression is still
present in the Western World. Atwood understands this
necessity, but also comprises the absurdity of American culture
in her novel. Even though Atwood satirizes them, Americans
need to understand the relevance of Offred's story. Every woman
should know and understand the three main struggles of
American feminism, find the parallels in The Handmaid's Tale,
then compare it to their own lives. Atwood's novel tells all
women to beware, take back their lives, and resist any
probability of a place like Gilead.

Notes

1. In terms of traditional dystopias such as George Orwell's 1984 and Aldous Huxley's *A Brave New World*, Amin Malak's essay postulates that *The Handmaid's Tale* meets all criteria for a dystopia, but Atwood adds the element of feminism and irony.

2. The peculiar title of Atwood's novel satirically deals with adult themes and patriarchal rankings. In Lucy M. Freibert's essay, she clarifies the title's meaning by saying, "The Chaucerian ring of the title sets up expectations of a medieval setting with lords and ladies, retainers and handmaids, a recounting of the battle of sexes from top to bottom of a hierarchal range, a latter-day Canterbury saga....The dual effect of the double-entendre in the pun on the word *tale*, as literary creation and anatomic part, combines humor and denigration..." (281).

3. Atwood claims that all aspects of Gilead are reflections of actual occurrences in the world. Rosemary Sullivan explains that Atwood kept a large fill of newspaper clippings about infertility in the mid-eighties. She also kept clippings about chemical pollution harming reproduction, cults, lead poisoning, toxic dumping, Agent Orange, and the now banned chemical pcbs (850). In her essay "'Just a Backlash': Margaret Atwood, Feminism, and *The Handmaid's Tale*", Jill Swale illuminates that Atwood also has a file on human and women's rights which she took on book tours to show that nothing was invented (859). Some of these clippings and manuscripts can be found in the Atwood Papers held in the University of Toronto's library.

4. In *The Handmaid's Tale*, Moira tries to escape the electric prod wielding Aunts, but she is recaptured and beaten on the feet with cables. Shirley Neuman points out that one of Atwood's clippings tells of Ayatollah Khomeini forcing women back into their traditional burqas, and Iranian refugees reported torture with electric cattle prods and frayed steel cables (859).

5. "Of-Fred" and "Of-Glen" satirize submission and slavery by using the possessive "of". In Jill Swale's essay, she explains Atwood's literary device when she states, "She has become a man's possession, belonging to Fred. This method of

naming is simply an extension of the Victorian tendency to refer to even eminent women, such as the writer Mrs. Humphry Ward, in terms of their husbands, and for slaves to take the surnames of their owners" (37). Lucy Freibert also concurs when she states that the possessive "Of" reinforces a slave context (283). Taking the literary device even further, David Coad states, "She is between red and off-red; she is off(e)red to (F)red" (no pag.).

Works Cited

Atwood, Margaret. *The Handmaid's Tale*. New York: Anchor, 1986. Print.

Coad, David. "Hymens, Lips and Masks: The Veil in Margaret Atwood's *The Handmaid's Tale*." *Literature and Psychology* 47.1 (2001): 54-67. Rpt. in *Contemporary Literature Criticism*. Vol. 246. Detroit: Gale, 54-67. *Literature Resource Center*. GALILEO. 15 Sept. 2009.

Freibert, Lucy M. "Control and Creativity: The Politics of Risk in Margaret Atwood's *The Handmaid's Tale*." *Critical Essays on Margaret Atwood*. Ed. Judith McCombs. Boston: Hall, 1998. 280-91. Print.

Malak, Amin. "Margaret Atwood's *The Handmaid's Tale* and the Dystopian Tradition." *The Handmaid's Tale*. Ed. and Introd. Harold Bloom. New York: Infobase, 2001. 3-10. Print.

Miner, Madonne. "'Trust Me': Reading the Romance Plot in Margaret Atwood's *The Handmaid's Tale*." *Twentieth Century Literature* 37.2 (1991): 148-68. *JSTOR*. GALILEO. Web. 4 Oct. 2009.

Napierkowski, Marie R, ed. "*The Handmaid's Tale*". *Novels for Students*. Vol. 4. Detroit: Gale, 1998. 114-38. *Gale Virtual Reference Library*. GALILEO. Web. 23 Sept. 2009.

Neuman, Shirley. "'Just a Backlash': Margaret Atwood, Feminism, and *The Handmaid's Tale*." *University of Toronto Quarterly* 75.3 (2006):857-67. *Project Muse*. GALILEO. Web. 15 Sept. 2009.

Rule, Lauren A. "Not Fading into Another Landscape: Specters of American Empire in Margaret Atwood's Fiction." *MFS [Modern Fiction Studies]* 54.4 (2008): 627-53. *Project Muse*. GALILEO. Web. 23 Sept. 2009.

Sullivan, Rosemary. "What If? Writing *The Handmaid's Tale*." *University of Toronto Quarterly* 75.3 (2006): 850-56. *Project Muse*. GALILEO. Web. 15 Sept. 2009.

Swale, Jill. "Feminism, and Politics in *The Handmaid's Tale*: Jill Swale Examines the Social and Historical Context of Atwood's Novel." *The English Review* 13.1 (2002):37. *Literature Resource Center*. GALILEO. Web. 24 Sept. 2009.

Contractors: Defeating Military Hunger at a Bargain

Philip Nethers
ENGL 1102H

♦♦♦

The War on Terror being fought in Iraq and Afghanistan, in which I participated, is happening in venues so distant from the United States as to initially seem unimaginable. The greater this separation from the home front and the battlefield, the higher the cost will be for the serving, transportation, and production of food for American soldiers. This distance creates an increased demand for cash to be sent into the ever hungry maw known as the military. As Napoleon Bonaparte is credited to have said, "An army travels on its stomach" (Alberts).

Until recently, the rule of thumb has been that the American army was expected to support itself in everything from providing shelter to feeding its troops. In the last fifty years, the amount of money needed for Congress to spend on the planning and execution required to feed America's army has skyrocketed. These rising costs have prompted the United States government to hire contractors to provide all food support for the military in lieu of keeping a self-sufficient armed force; this privatization of the military food support infrastructure has allowed the military to deploy itself in such a way that allows for more specific and specialized involvement in fighting and security without having to worry from where the next meal will come.

Militaries have classically been under public domain and controlled by the government. While this is still technically true, the United States has decided to include private companies in its armed force support structure. Even powerful U.S. allies such as the United Kingdom have seen the wisdom in this endeavor. For example, this idea of hiring "private contractors by the United Kingdom...was well established...by the late 1990s" (Uttley). This follows in the footsteps of the neo-American tradition of using contractors, the most powerful of these being Kellogg, Brown, and Root (KBR) which is "a [former] subsidiary of Halliburton, the Texas oil services giant" (Risen). The Logistics Civil Augmentation Program contract gave KBR the rights to become the principle food supporter of the United States military. To soldiers, this is a welcome change from the days when all food was made by army cooks. It also brings to mind Michael Schmitt's point that the "civilian footprint supporting military operations" has never been larger than in OIF (Calaguas). While this does put more civilians in harm's way, it is an unavoidable requirement of the efficiency that privatization brings to the military.

What is the reasoning behind his move towards relying on the private sector for support? Professor Steven Schooner reveals that supporting a standing army large enough to invade a country is very costly, but this cost can be offset by keeping a smaller military during peace time and bolstering it when needed with contractors that can be hired "very, very quickly at a rate we'd never be able to recruit [soldiers] otherwise" (Calaguas). These contractors would take "care of the food and the water...services" so that the military can focus on fighting instead of worrying about what is for dinner (Calaguas). This concept, known as surge capacity, shows the economic wisdom of using contractors instead of relying on a self-sufficient military where soldiers eat prepackaged Meals-Ready-To-Eat and unappetizing dehydrated food.

The government supports contractors when it takes into account the comparative costs of military support personnel and their civil analogues. While a soldier and a civilian can both cook, the civilian's specialization gives him a comparative advantage because of his lower opportunity cost; basically, the soldier can be used to fight while the civilian cannot. Because of the inequality of this cost and others favoring the private sector, the government is provided with an incentive to hire logistical contractors (Uttley). The open market in the private sector will create competition between contractors who need to accumulate profit; this will provide for an environment that will "exert a powerful discipline on private sector management and employees to maximize efficiency" (Uttley).

In order to better understand Congress' decision to privatize and hire KBR, here is an example that will help explain the extent of logistical food support provided by KBR. In just one dining facility (known as a DFAC) on the large Contingency Operating Base Speicher a few miles north of Baghdad, the team of army cooks and KBR employees has provided a total of "one million eight hundred thousand meals and counting..." (Alberts). This is only since the arrival of the current army unit does not include meals that any previous units provided for the troops at this location. To put it even more in perspective, this one DFAC "serves 12,000 meals a day...and half of those are delivered and served off-site at five remote dining locations on COB Speicher" (Alberts). While there are some soldiers helping run and oversee this operation, it would not be possible to provide this many meals without the support of KBR employees. If one were to calculate the amount of meals provided daily in every military DFAC in the Middle East, it becomes easier to understand why the government is willing to pay the seemingly exorbitant amount of $150 billion for its ten year contract with KBR (Risen).

While all this support would not be possible without KBR, the apparent wisdom of its contract has been questioned by many within the United States government who take notice of the copious fiscal abuses to which KBR has been attributed; there are several cases where KBR has blatantly mismanaged its resources, costing the United States government billions of dollars. In 2004, "army auditors had determined that KBR lacked credible data or records" (Risen) for some accounts of fraud and waste concerning food. One of the contributors to this problem arose when KBR served ruined and expired food to soldiers in Iraq. According to Rory Mayberry, the former KBR Food Production Manager, this was a common practice. He describes KBR procedures for food trucks that were shot and or bombed while in a convoy: "we were told to go into the trucks…and use [the food] after removing the bullets and any shrapnel…. [If] the military turn[ed] the food items away,… KBR just sent the food to another base for use" (Major Findings). Although this would never have been allowed by United States army cooks in a self-sufficient military, it does not compare to the benefits added by KBR; indeed, even soldier morale would decrease if KBR were not used because, according to Sergeant Sean Wroten, a good meal might be the only things that soldiers can anticipate on any given day (Alberts).

The U.S. government is no stranger to food waste and fraud of its own. Although some of these are not directly food related, they do give one a good sense of how the government would mismanage food resources if given the chance. For example, the Pentagon is owner to the blaring abuses of having failed to provide correct oversight to KBR in its $1.8 billion fiasco. Although this debacle included a KBR abuse of requisitioning "a big-screen TV and lots of food for the private use of" its employees" for a Super Bowl party, according to Julie McBride, the former KBR Morale, Welfare and Recreation Officer (Major Findings), fraud in the United States executive branch allowed this to occur. Dick Cheney, the vice president during this era, had "previously served as [Halliburton's] chief executive" (Risen) and was most likely the driving force for the government quickly outsourcing its contracting audit requirements when its own auditors recommended suspending payments to KBR (Major Findings). This knowledge clearly shows that there is waste from the public and private pieces of the military.

Abuses and waste have been plentiful on both sides of the business relationship between the United States government and KBR. Since there is no clear difference between public and private food support in this area, it cannot be used to decide whether to hire KBR or another contractor or to stick with the original self-sufficient military. Thus, one must look at the other mitigating factors such as increased efficiency provided by contractors and the ability to enact surge capacity at a moment's notice. A third factor is the morale boost from food items such as steaks, stir fry, and ice cream provided by contractors; spirits would drop quickly if soldiers were forced to return to dehydrated and prepackaged foods. With all of this in mind, it becomes apparent that the better option is to stick with the contractors for food services and the increased efficiency that they provide. If the Pentagon were to exercise all contractual food logistical support, then all the abuses and waste would then come from the military. This public cost would then be multiplied because of the lost economic benefits of having specialized civilians providing food and other logistical support. Clearly, when it comes to providing food for the military, contractors are the correct choice. Why force troops to eat only dehydrated and prepackaged food when better alternatives are available at a lower long run cost to the government.

Works Cited

Alberts, Mike. "TF Wing's DFAC Soldiers Attention to Detail, Cooperation Key to Food Service Success." 2 April 2010. *USA.gov.* Web. 7 April 2011.

Calaguas, Mark. "Military Privatization: Efficiency or Anarchy?" *Chi-Kent J. Int'l & Comp.* 2006. 58-81. Web. 10 April 2011.

"Major Findings: DPC Oversight Hearings on Waste, Fraud, and Corruption in Iraq." 26 September 2010. *USA.gov.* Web. 10 April 2011.

Risen, James. "Army overseer tells of ouster over KBR stir." *New York Times.* 17 June 2008. *Opposing Viewpoints.* Web. 18 Apr. 2011.

Uttley, Matthew R. H. "Private contractors on deployed operations: the United Kingdom experience." *Defence Studies.* 4.2 (2004): 145-165. *Academic Search Complete.* Web. 18 April 2011.

***

Why I Like This Essay: I admire Philip Nethers' essay "Contractors: Defeating Military Hunger at a Bargain" because the topic is so original and so relevant. Phil was able to focus the general topic of "Food and Politics" that I assigned his English 1102 Honors class into one specific to his experience as a soldier. That was no small task. His essay reminds readers--without ever sounding didactic or sentimental--of the logistical reality of war. And he uses his sources so well, a great example being that he quantifies the number of meals (over 12,000) that only one military base in Afghanistan prepares each day. As a result, his main argument resonates into a much more important argument about not just the cost of war, but the importance of providing troops such small morale boosters as decent meals. His writing is compelling. The essay is smart, well-researched, and interesting, subtly conveying Phil's passion for his topic. It reads like an essay that he wanted to write, rather than one that he had to write.

Anna Schachner, Associate Professor of English

The Heroism of Paul Rusesabagina: A Character Study of George's *Hotel Rwanda*

Chiemeka Ugochukwu
ENGL 1102H

◆◆◆

Outline

Thesis: In *Hotel Rwanda,* Paul Rusesabagina's initial reluctance to help others during the 1994 Rwanda genocide changing into zeal to save every Rwandan is instigated by his realization that the conflict is severe, his courageous sense of morality and justice, and his desire for a future for Rwanda.

I. Paul realizes that the conflict is severe.

    A. How the conflict commenced.

        1. The conflict in Rwanda gradually commenced.

        2. The conflict then became instantaneous with escalation of hostilities.

    B. The realization of the intensity of the conflict caused Paul's immediate change in attitude.

        1. He initially refuses to accept the fact that there will soon be a major conflict in Rwanda.

        2. He later realizes the intensity of the conflict and swiftly changes his attitude.

II. Paul is the epitome of the true image of morality and justice.
   A. The history of injustice in Rwanda began through colonization.
      1. The Belgian colonists favored the Tutsis over the Hutus.
      2. The Belgian colonists used the Tutsis as an instrument of oppression over the Hutus.
   B. Paul's courage, morality, and leadership skills are demonstrated during the genocide.
      1. Paul's high sense of morality is exhibited when he saves both the Hutus and the Tutsis in spite of what history says.
      2. Paul has the courage to stand for what is right despite the impending dangers to his life and his family.
      3. Paul's unwavering leadership skills are also demonstrated throughout the events that happened during the genocide.
III. Paul wants a future for his country.
   A. Paul's love for his family and respect for his community is exemplified in the movie.
      1. He hopes for a better future for his family.
      2. He aspires for a community where ethnicity does not matter.
   B. Paul hopes for a better country.
      1. He hopes for everything to return to normal.
      2. He aspires for a great Rwanda.

It is common knowledge that whenever natural resources of value are found in any part of Africa, conflict erupts. In Rwanda, however, this was not the case. Unlike Nigeria that has crude oil and Sierra Leone that has diamonds, both of which have experienced their own share of conflict, Rwanda has no major natural resources of particular interest to the world. This was where the bloodiest genocide ever experienced in the history of Africa took place. According to Rene Lemarchand, over eight hundred thousand lives of men, women, and children were taken (307). The way they were killed can only be imagined. The obvious question is what was the reason behind this outrageous killing? According to Paul Rusesabagina, racial hatred was the driving force behind the killings (x).

Rwanda is comprised of three major ethnic groups, the Hutus, the Tutsis, and the Twas. In the words of David Newbury, "Rwanda population includes several broad social categories: Hutu (85%), Tutsi (14%) and Twa (1%), as well as narrower identities of region, clan, and lineage" (78). Since the Hutus and the Tutsis are the major ethnic groups in that country, the conflict was mostly between them. The relationship of these ethnic groups was amiable until the arrival of the colonists. Kenneth W. Harrow describes how the German and the Belgian colonists invaded Rwanda, imposing identity card and fixed identity legal status on them. He further describes how the Belgian colonists favored the Tutsi ethnic group, giving them control over political and economical affairs (223). This created animosity between the ethnic groups which was carried on from generation to generation until it resulted in a full-fledged genocide.

The story of the Rwandan genocide is told in Terry George's movie *Hotel Rwanda.* In describing the director, Anne Thompson says that George is an Irishman with an aptitude for taking difficult stories to the screen. Among his numerous films are *In the Name of the Father, The Boxer,* and *Some Mother's Son*[1] in which he made his directing debut (47). Indeed, bringing the story of the genocide to the world through film could be an uphill task. Thompson writes that George was set to tackle the difficulty of telling an African story; he did not want to elaborate on the horror of the genocide, but he also did not want to soften it either. Thompson says that George decided to turn the movie into a love story of a husband and wife who save not only their family, but as many people as they can from definite death (48). The movie is excellent in that George uses a less known story of how a hotel manager saved the lives of others to tell a widely known tale of the Rwandan genocide.

In Terry George's *Hotel Rwanda,* Paul Rusesabagina, uses his position and influence as house manager of the prestigious Miles Collines Hotel in Rwanda to save his family and more than a thousand refugees from being killed in the raging genocide that was in progress in the country. Paul, a Hutu, married to Tatiana, a Tutsi, was one man who stood to make a difference risking his life and that of his family to save as many people as he could from the ongoing slaughter of the Tutsi's by the Hutus. Paul was initially reluctant to help out from the onset of the event. He had a personal philosophy that only family members should be helped. He explains this to Tatiana his wife when she tries to persuade him to help Victor, a good neighbor, who was arrested by the police. He says, "He's not family. Family is all that matters" (Pearson and George 16). Of course, this philosophy spontaneously changes following events during the genocide. In *Hotel Rwanda*, Paul Rusesabagina's initial reluctance to help others during the 1994 Rwandan genocide changing into zeal to save every Rwandan is instigated by his realization that the conflict is severe, his courageous sense of morality and justice, and his desire for a future for Rwanda.

The fact that the conflict in Rwanda started slowly might be a testament to Paul's failure to realize the severity of the conflict. According to Harrow, the origin of the conflict can be traced back to the Hutu revolution of 1959 against the Belgian colonists who used the Tutsis as instruments of governance and consequently oppression. The Hutus ascended to power with the independence of the nation in 1962, causing a shift in Belgian policies, decentering[2] of Tutsis from positions of power, and the rise of Hutu nationalism under Kayibanda[3] (223). Due to Kayibanda's social revolution and ethnic purges, most Tutsis fled to Uganda; they subsequently formed the Rwanda Patriotic Front (RPF) to attack Rwanda. Harrow explains that because there was a response to the plea of Rwanda for military assistance against the RPF by the French, there became pressures by the international community on Rwanda to form a multiparty democracy and bring the opposition into negotiation; this was in the late 1980s and 1990s (224). In "'Train Peut En Cacher Un Autre': Narrating the Rwanda Genocide and *Hotel* Rwanda," Harrow accurately explains what happens next: "Then comes the reprise of Hutu nationalism, Hutu extremism, Radio Miles Collines and the machinations of Madame Habyarimana[4], her northern clan, and the sympathetic army officers. Finally begins the work of the death squads up north, requiring a sidebar to consider the impact and demands of the RPF" (224). Harrow writes that following the invasion of Rwanda by the RPF in 1990, president Habyarimana decided to sign the Arusha accords[5]. He says there were repeated threats by the RPF in 1992, and then there was the intervention of the French troops in 1993. The conflict finally escalated when the plane carrying the President was shot down on April 6, 1994 (224).

In *Hotel Rwanda*, Paul refuses to accept the fact that there might soon be a major conflict in Rwanda. This is arguably due to the fact that Rwanda has seen a lot of conflicts over the past decades, and the President has just signed a major agreement with the rebels that will settle the conflict. In the movie, Thomas and Fedens, Paul's in-laws, come to him hours before the President's plane is shot down, expressing fears of a major conflict in the country. Paul dismisses this fear, saying that the United Nations and the whole world are watching and that the peace agreement has just been signed. He is, of course, wrong because just as the conversation continues, the President's plane is shot down, and conflict erupts. Paul pacifies his in-laws, telling them to come to his house in the morning to discuss the issue in greater detail. Paul's refusal to accept the facts brought forth by his in-laws is conceivably because he desperately wants peace for his country. Being in a country that has been in darkness for a long time, Paul latches onto any shimmering of light that shines on the country no matter how dim or fickle it seems. Even as he drives back home from work, he sees violence ensuing all around him, but he still refuses to believe that anything is wrong.

Perhaps, the turning point for Paul is when the Rwandan soldiers come to his house to take him; they want him to retrieve the keys of the Hotel Diplomat, where he formerly worked, from a safe. When prompted to follow the soldiers, Paul refuses to follow them unless his family goes with him. He initially opts to take only his family along, but due to the persuasion of his wife, Paul takes everyone who had come to his house for protection. This is the beginning of his heroic acts. While trying to get the keys inside, the captain of the Rwandan soldiers finds out that the people Paul brings along are Tutsis. In rage the captain puts a gun to Paul's head and says, "Shoot them or you die first" (Pearson and George 34). Paul then successfully persuades the captain to take money instead of the lives of the innocent people. The reason for Paul's change in attitude is that he realizes the gravity of the conflict. He sees the horror in progress around him, and even though he is pushed to some extent by his wife, Paul himself realizes that the people who run to him need a savior, and if he turns them back, they will be slaughtered.

There are so many reasons why Paul should refuse to help the Tutsis who run to him. The major reason can be found in the history of Rwanda, the very reason for the conflict. According to Lemarchand the reason is because of the "…Historic 'victimization of the Hutu masses of Rwanda at the hands of the Tutsi monarchy, [that are] ultimately rendered all the more painful by the constraints and discriminations introduced by colonial overrule" (307). The Belgian colonists chose the Tutsi clan to the Hutu tribe because they presumably looked more like them and were more elegant. Thompson states, "…The Belgians at first chose the dominant Tutsi tribes, who were land-owning herders, to be their managerial ruling class because they were supposedly more "European" -looking, with thinner lips and noses and finer hair" (48). The nepotism introduced by the colonists was the cause of the tribalism that happened in Rwanda; it was the very foundation of the genocide. When the Belgians left, there was an overthrow of government, and the Hutus took control of government. The Hutus then sought revenge for the years of oppression, and in 1994 their revenge was enacted in the bloodiest manner ever.

In the film, Paul, who is fully aware of Rwanda's history and the reason for the genocide, chooses to save both the Hutus and the Tutsi regardless of what history says. He exhibits his high sense of morality when he chooses to do what is right and allow all who can make it to the Hotel to come in notwithstanding their tribe. Perhaps, his high sense of morality leads him to the delusion that everyone must act like he does, and that the western world, the people he so admires, will step in and save them because of the atrocities being committed there. In the movie when Paul talks with Jack, the journalist, he thanks him for taking footage of what was really going on in Rwanda in the hopes that the western world will see this and act. He is, however, shocked by Jack's reply. Jack says, "I think if people see this footage, they'll say, 'Oh my God, that's horrible,' and then go on eating their dinners" (Pearson and George 54). Paul is surprised at this statement because he believes that the western world, more than any other people, should know the true meaning of morality, even more than he does. This, nevertheless, does little to eradicate Paul's sense of morality as he works away from Jack, going on to do his job organizing the hotel.

Another major theme of *Hotel Rwanda* is Paul's courage to stand for what is right despite impending dangers to his life, and his family. Anthere Nzabatsinda in "Hotel Rwanda" explains the risk Paul is in:

> The film opens on a radio propaganda (Hutu Power Radio) in which the announcer exhorts Hutus to "stay alert," "watch [their] neighbors," the Tutsis, who are referred to as "cockroaches," "traitors," and "invaders"; they are suspected of secretly helping the RPF (Rwanda Patriotic Front) soldiers, "the Rebels," in combating the Hutu regime, army, and militia General Juvenal Habyarimana, a Hutu dictator who was president of Rwanda since 1973, has just been killed as his plane was downed near Kigali-Rwanda airport. The radio is accusing the Rebels of having assassinated the Hutu president. This assassination has been the triggering moment for the official government army aided by all mad

militiamen (the "Interahamwe," Those-who-work-Together) to kill all the Tutsis they could as well as the Hutus in opposition to Habyarimana regime. Paul Rusesabagina is a Hutu but is deemed sympathetic to Tutsis, for his wife Tatiana (Sophie Okonedo) is a Tutsi. Therefore, Paul is himself threatened. (235)

In the movie, after the foreign soldiers who come to take only foreign nationals, leave, the Rwandan militia comes to evacuate everybody in the hotel. Paul shows his courage by convincing the soldiers to wait for a while, buying time while he makes desperate calls to the General and to Tillens (the president of Sabina and owner of the Hotel). Even more pronounced is his audacity to mock the soldiers' intelligence by giving them the guest list containing foreigners only from two weeks before instead of giving them the current guest list that contains the names of all the Hutus and Tutsis in his hotel when he is asked to provide the guest list. This he does to prevent the separation of Hutus from Tutsis and the consequent massacre of all the Tutsis in his hotel. His courage pays off as the owner of the hotel calls the French President who conceivably calls the General of the Army who orders the soldiers out of the hotel.

Paul's unwavering leadership skills are also demonstrated throughout the events that happened during the genocide. A major climax of his leadership skills in *Hotel Rwanda* is when he gives a moving speech to everyone in the hotel after the owner of the hotel tells him there will be no rescue:

> There will be no rescue. No intervention force. We can only save ourselves. Many of you know influential people abroad. You must call these people. You must tell them what will happen to us. Say good bye. But when you say goodbye, say it as though you are reaching through the phone and holding their hand. Let them know that if they let go of that hand... you will die. We must shame them into sending help. Most importantly, this can not be a refugee camp. The Interahamwe believe that the Mille Collines is a

four-star Sabena hotel. That is the only thing
keeping us alive. (Pearson and George 77)
Paul then goes around organizing the hotel and makes sure that
the hotel continues to function as a four star hotel. This
undoubtedly shows his impeccable leadership qualities.

Finally, even though Paul is portrayed as a Hero in *Hotel
Rwanda*, his most desirable quality, and perhaps his major
driving force, is his desire for a future for Rwanda. He hopes for
a better future for his family, and he aspires for a community
where ethnicity does not matter. In *Hotel Rwanda*, while Paul is
packing some whiskey and jewels for General Bizimungu, the
general begins to tell him about the wonderful experience he had
in Scotland and how he wonders if he will ever return. When he
asks Paul if he thinks he will return, Paul replies, "I hope we all
get to do a great many things General…" (Pearson and George
112). Even when given an offer to leave with the General to
Gitarama, the new army headquarters, Paul refuses, opting to get
his family instead. This shows Paul's love for his family, and
indeed the community as whole, and his desire for a great future
for Rwanda. Paul hopes that everything will return to normal,
and that Rwanda will eventually rise again. He implies this when
finally leaving the hotel; he says, "I hope someday we will come
back" (Pearson and George 119).

The way Terry George presents the story of the
Rwandan genocide to the world is indeed impeccable. The
reluctance of Paul being turned to zeal was inspired by the
severity of the conflict, his courageous sense of morality and
justice, and his desire for a future for Rwanda. Although there
are a lot of controversies as to the heroism of the real Paul
Rusesabagina,[6] the fact of the matter is that one man stood to
make a difference when everybody backed down. Over a
thousand people live to this day because of the deed of one man.
In describing the reception Rusesabagina and his wife received
when they came back for the first time since they left Rwanda,
George says, "As he stepped off the plane in Kigali, Paul was
mobbed by friends and family. At the Mille Collines Hotel, the
staff rushed to hug the man who had saved their lives.
Everywhere we went, Paul and Tatiana were greeted as heroes"
(24). Paul's hope for a better future is slowly becoming a reality

as Rwanda has seen a significant improvement in the economy and welfare of its population since the genocide. In describing the remarkable recovery of Rwanda An Ansoms says, "Rwanda's post-conflict economic recovery seems to be a story of extraordinary success after a pervasive period of civil war and genocide" (496). Ansoms explains that unlike other countries that have been through conflict and has seen a war overhang effect, Rwanda's economy has been one of steady growth (497). Rwanda's remarkable recovery is evidence that the people of Rwanda have learned from their horrific past. Ethnicity has been put aside, and killers and victims have come together to build a better Rwanda, a Rwanda that Paul Rusesabagina envisaged.

Notes

1.   *Some Mother's Son* was the film Terry George used to make his directing debut. It is a wrenching film about the 1980's hunger strike done by the Northern Irish women that had their sons imprisoned by the British Army (Thompson 47).

2.   Kenneth Harrow uses the word "decentering" to show the change of the mantle of leadership from the Tutsis to the Hutus (223).

3.   According to one source, "Kayibanda Gregoire, 1924-76, [was a] political leader in Rwanda. A Hutu, he worked as a journalist and later founded the Ruanda (now Rwanda) cooperative Movement (1952), the Hutu Social Movement (1957), and the Democratic Republican Movement (1959). In 1961 he became president of Rwanda. He was overthrown in an army coup just before the 1973 elections" ("Gregoire Kayibanda").

4.   One source states, "Agathe Habyarimana (born Agathe Kanziga in 1942) is the widow of former president of Rwanda Juvenal Hanyarimana. Kanziga is part of a Hutu lineage that long ruled an independent principality until the late nineteenth century. She was arrested by French authorities on 2 March, 2010, in France following the French president Nicolas Sarkozy's visit to Rwanda" ("Agathe Habyarimana").

5.   According to Lindsay Scorgie the Arusha Accords – signed on August 3, 1993 by Rwanda's two warring factions, the Government of Rwanda (GoR) and the Rwandan Patriotic Front (RPF) – are an extraordinary testament to the fact that even the most well-crafted negotiation cannot be considered an accomplishment until implemented (Scorgie 66).

6. The then president of Rwanda, Paul Kageme, disliked *Hotel Rwanda* for being an inaccurate depiction of the conflict. During the genocide, Kageme was the leader of the RPF forces that eventually brought the bloodshed to an end. While deeming the film "useful in bringing the plight of Rwanda" to the attention of the world community, he disputes the claim that Paul Rusesabagina having saved so many became like a hero. He says, "Paul Rusesabagina did not save people. He had no means to do it, and he did not do it." Kagame went on to claim that a trade off was negotiated by which his [Kagame's] forces allowed

those stranded in the hotel to go. "He himself tried to escape and was turned back," he added of Rusesabagina. Kagame's remarks represent a growing sentiment among some people in Rwanda who reject the notion that Rusesabagina is a hero (Uraizee 17).

Works Cited

"Agathe Habyarimana." *Wikipedia*. Wikipedia Foundation Inc, 20 Oct 2010. Web. 30 Dec 2010.

Ansoms, An. "Ressurection after Civil War and Genocide: Growth, Poverty and Inequality in Post-conflict Rwanda." *European Journal of development Research* 17.3 (2005): 495-508. *Academic Search Complete.* Web. 30 Nov. 2010.

George, Terry. "My Promise." Hotel Rwanda. *Bringing the True Story of an African Here to Film.* Terry George and Keir Pearson. New York: Newmarket, 2005. 23-29. Print.

"Gregoire Kayibanda." *Columbia Electronic Encyclopedia,* 2010. *Academic Search Complete.* Web. 30 Nov. 2010.

Harrow, Kenneth W. "'Un Train Peut En Cacher Un Autre': Narrating the Rwanda Genocide and *Hotel Rwanda.*" Rev. of *Hotel Rwanda,* dir. Terry George. *Research in African Literatures* 36.4. (2005): 223-32. *MLA International Bibliography.* Web. 2 Oct 2010.

Hotel Rwanda. Dir. Terry George. By Keir Pearson. Perf. Don Cheadle and Sophie Okonedo. MGM Home Entertainment, 2004. DVD.

Lemarchand, Rene. "A History of Genocide in Rwanda." *Journal of African History* 43.2 (2002): 307-11. *JSTOR.* Web. 28 Sept. 2010.

Newbury, David. "Understanding Genocide." *African Studies Review* 41.1 (1998): 73-97. *JSTOR.* Web. 28 Sept. 2010.

Nzabatsinda, Anthere. "*Hotel Rwanda,*" Rev. of *Hotel Rwanda,* dir. Terry George. *Research in African Literatures* 36.4 (2005): 233-36. *Film and Television Literature Index.* Web. 2 Oct. 2010.

Pearson, Keir, and George Terry. "The Screenplay." Hotel Rwanda. *Bringing the True Story of an African Here to Film.* Terry George and Keir Pearson. New York: Newmarket, 2005. 117-244. Print.

Rusesabagina, Paul. Introduction. *An Ordinary Man: An Autobiography.* Paul Rusesabagina and Tom Zoellner. New York: Viking, 2006. ix-xvi. Print.

Scorgie, Lindsay. "Rwanda's Arusha Accords: A Missed Opportunity." *Undercurrent* 1.1 (2004): 66-76. *Academic Search Complete.* Web. 30 Nov. 2010.

Thompson, Anne. "The Struggle of Memory Against Forgetting." Hotel Rwanda: *Bringing the True Story of an African Hero to Film.* Terry George and Keir Pearson. New York: Newmarket, 2005. 47-59. Print.

Uraizee, Joya. "Grazing at the Beast: Describing Mass Murder in Deepa Mehta's *Earth* and Terry George's *Hotel Rwanda." An Interdisciplinary Journal of Jewish Studies* 28.4 (2010): 10-27. *Academic Search Complete.* Web. 28 Sept. 2010.

Innocence Lost, Understanding Obtained

Taneka Hightower
ENGL 2131

◆◆◆

The slave narrative is a work created by an African American who was a slave who either ran away or purchased his or her freedom. These written works were created to draw attention to the horrific times of slavery, humanize slave characters, shed light on Christian ideals that were often times contradicted, and/or highlight the mistreatment of slaves by their owners. Within each narrative, there is a framework known as the four chronological phases of plot. Of these phases, the loss of innocence phase is vital to help connect the reader to the character and convey the author's message within the work. The loss of innocence has an important function in the slave narrative and has influenced the revisionist project of the neo-slave narrative.

In her book, *Witnessing Slavery: The Development of Ante-bellum Slave Narratives,* Frances Smith Foster describes the four chronological phases of plot and gives a brief description of them and their purpose. The first is "the loss of innocence" (85). She explains that this is the moment when slaves become aware that they are a slave. They also learn what it really means to be a slave. Next, there is "the realization of alternatives to bondage and the formulation of a resolve to be free" (85). Foster declares this as the moment when the protagonist decides he or she will no longer be a slave and will obtain freedom. Third is "the escape," which is the moment that he or she does just that. Lastly, there is "freedom obtained," which is the moment when the slave gains his or her freedom (85). Foster indicates that this format is based on principles and ideas of Christianity which influenced what slaves believed and how they dealt with their circumstance. It is a truly traumatic experience for the protagonists to learn of their enslavement. The reader's realization that the ignorance and then knowledge of slaves that they are indeed a slave is vital to many works in the African American tradition. Laurie G. Kirszner and Stephen R. Mandell discuss the loss of innocence themes used by African American and Latino writers and give some examples of why they are used:

> ...loss of innocence may be presented as a first encounter with racial prejudice; a conflict between the individual and society ... a conflict between a minority view and the values of the dominate group; ... failure or aborted relationships may revolve around language difficulties or cultural misunderstanding. (4)

They explain the author's intended use of the loss of innocence phase. In the slave narrative, many of these aspects are addressed while showing the protagonist's individual loss of innocence. These can be in the form of an act upon them or just witnessing an act on someone else. No matter what form the loss of innocence takes, it assists in conveying the message to the reader that the author is trying to present about the particular character.

In some works, such as the slave narrative *Incidents in the Life of a Slave Girl,* the loss of innocence occurs because of a clear contradiction related to Christian beliefs which leads to betrayal. At the age of twelve, Harriet Jacobs' mistress died. Jacobs knew that her mistress promised her mother on her death bed that Jacobs and her siblings would "never suffer for any thing" (283). Subsequently, she was given to her mistress' niece, "a child of five years of age" (283). Harriet recalled:

> My mistress had taught me the precepts of
> God's Word: 'Thou shalt love thy neighbor as
> thyself.' But I was her slave, and I suppose she
> did not recognize me as her neighbor. I would
> give much to blot out from my memory that one
> great wrong...I try to think with less bitterness
> of this act of injustice. (Jacobs 283)

Jacobs expresses to the reader that she had been betrayed, and she wishes that this memory could be erased from her mind. Her feelings of sadness and disappointment help her to show the reader just how immoral it was for her to be a slave. Not only is it immoral, but it is hypocritical to what her mistress taught her which were said to be "God's Words."

True to the slave narrative form, Frederick Douglas shares his loss of innocence in a vivid account of his aunt being whipped for disobeying her master:

> Before he commenced whipping Aunt Hester, he
> took her into the kitchen, and stripped her from
> neck to waist, leaving her neck, shoulders, and
> back, entirely naked. . . . [H]e commenced to lay
> on the heavy cowskin, and soon the warm, red
> blood (amid heart-rending shrieks from her, and
> horrid oaths from him) came dripping to the
> floor. I was so terrified and horror-stricken at the
> sight, that I hid myself in a closet, and dared not
> venture out till long after the bloody transaction
> was over. I expected it would be my turn next...
> I had never seen anything like it before. (398)

Douglas' loss of innocence in witnessing his aunt being beaten is truly a shocking experience for him. He has never observed such cruelty and mistreatment and begins to realize that enslavement means that a slave can be treated however the master sees fit. He is so traumatically affected by witnessing this account of abuse and degradation that he is fearful that he will also be punished and hides himself in a closet. The vivid description Douglas depicts causes a reader to directly feel sympathy for him as well as Aunt Hester. He has had no real idea that he belonged to someone who can treat people like animals and beat them worse than a dog that disobeys its master.

Slave narratives are not the only works of literature that use the loss of innocence to stir up the emotions of the audience. In contemporary literature, there has been an emergence of the neo-slave narrative. In a book titled, *Neo-Slave Narratives: Studies in the Social of a Literary Form,* Ashraf H.A. Rushby defines neo slave narratives as "contemporary novels that assume the form, adopt the conventions, and take on the first-person voice of the antebellum slave narrative" (3). Rushby's definition helps to clarify the progression of the loss of innocence concept from slave narratives to a more modern world of literature. Furthermore, the neo-slave narrative assists in trying to explain the gaps in history that are not even acknowledged in the antebellum narratives. Lawrence Hill's neo slave narrative explores the loss of innocence from a different perspective than the antebellum narratives. In his novel, *Someone Knows My Name* (2007)*,* he uses his character, Aminata Diallo, to present the loss of innocence as a disconnection from religion. This idea is definitely contemporary in comparison to the antebellum loss of innocence because Aminata loses her religion that she was born with while in Africa. Aminata is a devoted Muslim and believes that she can be spared enslavement because of this fact. Once she is enslaved, she soon learns that this is false, and she loses her faith. As a young child, Aminata believes, "…no Muslim was allowed to hold another Muslim in captivity. She says, "I believed that I would be safe" (Hill 13). Upon being captured she says, "This is a mistake," I said. "I am a freeborn Muslim. Let me go!"…I hoped that someone would hear the words in Arabic and realize the mistake. But nobody heard me. Or cared" (25). Once she arrives in Sullivan Island, she states, "I am cold, and I can't even pray. Allah doesn't live here (94). After spending time in the new world Aminata declares, "Praying inside my head felt lonely and futile. As the nights came and went, thoughts of Allah faded" (107). These excerpts show how Aminata thought that she would be protected by her faith and soon learns that this was not of any importance to her captors. Throughout the story, a reader can feel Aminata's depression and sadness because her faith did not permit her salvation. Eventually, she completely disconnects herself from her Muslim beliefs, and her faith is completely diminished by the experience of being enslaved. Hill's use of religious disconnection as the loss of innocence is a revision of the traditional slave narrative of the antebellum era. Traditionally, the religion of slaves was Christianity. However, Hill presents a quite controversial concept that has been disputed for years about Africans who were captured and taken into slavery not being cultured and having no religion until they were introduced to Christianity. Hill's modification to the religion scheme of the novel helps readers to understand the importance of the neo-slave narratives' attempt to account for the moments in history which are not represented.

The loss of innocence phase has assisted slave narratives in impacting society with the dramatic memories of former slaves. It also coaches the neo-slave narrative in its effort to account for lost moments in time that are not always presented in antebellum narratives because of the limitations imposed on those authors by their society. The revision of the loss of innocence ideal assists contemporary literature in answering unanswered questions about what the slaves felt and what went on during slavery. Not only does it fill in the gaps, but it allows modern writers to do research and present the world with new, more accurate ideas than those of the traditional slave narrative. The loss of innocence concept is still used in contemporary writing to draw in unsuspecting audiences and to reveal the historical truths about slavery that still affect us today.

Works Cited

Douglas, Frederick. *Narrative of the Life of Frederick Douglas.*
    Norton Anthology of African American Literature. Eds.
    Henry Louis Gates, Jr. and Nellie Y. McKay et al. 2nd ed.
    New York: Norton, 2004. 387-452. Print.

Foster, Frances Smith. *Witnessing Slavery: The Development of*
    Ante-bellum Slave Narratives. 2nd ed. Madison: U of
    Wisconsin P, 1979. Print.

Hill, Lawrence. *Someone Knows My Name.* New York: Norton,
    2007. Print.

Jacobs, Harriet. from *Incidents in the Life of a Slave Girl. Norton*
    Anthology of African American Literature. Eds. Henry
    Louis Gates, Jr. and Nellie Y. McKay et al. 2nd ed. New
    York: Norton, 2004. 280-315. Print.

Kirszner, Laurie G. and Stephen R. Mandell. *Fiction: Reading,*
    Reacting, Writing. Orlando: Harcourt Brace, 1994. Print.

Rushdy, Ashraf H. A. *Neo-Slave Narratives: Studies in the*
    Social of a Literary Form. New York: Oxford, 1999.
    Print.

***

Why I Like This Essay: Taneka's essay is a wonderful example
of the kind of scholarship we would like students to aspire to in
sophomore-level literature courses. This essay pulls together
important concepts, themes, and critics presented in this special
topics course on African American literature and adeptly
synthesizes and applies them to relevant pieces of literature. She
does a good job of narrowing her topic and selecting good
examples from the primary sources so that she can concisely
analyze three major works in one short essay. She also sets up a
solid theoretical framework for approaching her analysis. Great
work!

Dr. Valerie Dotson, Associate Professor of English

How the Females Once Wept:
Transgressions of the Female Mulatto Slave

Hendry Kurniawan
ENGL 2131

◆◆◆

The idea of womanhood once only stood as a mere representation of degradation and dehumanization. This stigma dominated the life of a female slave in the antebellum era of the late 1800s. Exposure to sexual violations was the norm for these female slaves as their masters laid their hands upon the spirit of the innocent. The life of slavery was more than a crime in itself, but to have a woman suffer the series of ill-fated events born from her sex, her identity from God himself, is an unfathomable thought even in the far reaches of the human imagination. Such was no exception when it came to the literary works of Harriet Jacobs's "Incidents in the Life of a Slave Girl" and William Wells Brown's "Clotel; or, The President's Daughter." The degree of sinful violations casted upon these females is immeasurable as seen from the details of these two literary works, for they bring to the forefront details that rapture the mind, allowing for complete understanding of the torturous life of a female slave. Taking into account both iconic literary works, the experiences of being a female slave were propelled into the spotlight as the work of William Wells Brown and Harriet Jacobs depicts events that are intrinsically attached to a life of a mulatto slave girl.

Being a mulatto slave girl, one is bound to have some form of relationship with the dominant male figure. These relationships are rarely positive as seen in "Incidents in the Life of a Slave Girl" and "Clotel; or, The President's Daughter." Linda Brent, the pseudonym used in place of Harriet Jacobs, had a white lover named Mr. Sands, whom she had children with; however, knowing all too well the injustices of a female slave, Sand disowned Linda Brent. Along with being a female slave, Brent is now a single mother all on her own. Such a life was common in the plight of a slave girl. Similarly, Brown depicted a parallel event that occurred in Clotel's life as Horatio Green, Clotel's husband, forsakes her for his job as a politician and his new wife. Seeing from these tragic examples, the life of a female mulatto harbored no great benefits. Linda Brent epitomizes this role to perfection as Dr. Flint, her previous owner and rapist, "had sworn that he would make [her] suffer, to [her] last day" (Jacobs 294). Slaves were mere possessions in the times of the late 1800s. Rational thinking would make one realize that possessions should be taken cared for, not beaten and looked down upon. Both of these female slaves have encountered dominant male figures in their life, and both struck relationships with their lovers, but to no avail, the relationships never settled on the bliss essence of love and care.

The damaged relationship that Linda Brent and Clotel were engaged in only brought forth a sense of individuality, growing stronger as prominent female figures in a patriarchal society. Such strength was exemplified when Brent stood by her morals in regards for her daughter as "[Brent] wanted no chain to be fastened on [her] daughter, not even if its links were of gold" (Jacobs 295). Brent never wanted her daughter to experience the chains of slavery; therefore, Brent did not take this golden chain her master bestowed upon wholeheartedly. This was Brent's way to try to protect her baby from the realities of the world. This zeal reigned true also for Clotel as parallelism strikes the two characters. After the separation from Horatio Green, Clotel also emotionally separated herself from the equation, for even

Green's "gold watch and chain were all laid aside as if no value" to her (Brown 339). The gold watch symbolizes wealth and memories of Green time have instilled, but even Clotel, a poor slave girl, seamlessly ignores the value and proclaims her stature as a strong individual. Jacobs and Brown tell their stories in great detail, yet no matter how detailed the stories are, both authors still coherently depict the same experiences exemplified through the parallelisms described between Brent and Clotel. Though these characters are different in their own ways, the bonds they share are forever. The bond of womanhood in the life of a slave girl is the constant backdrop for the experiences these females had to suffer.

By having relationships and encounters with these male figures, Linda Brent and Clotel consequently undergo demoralizing exposure to sexual violations from these slave masters. Being both very beautiful mulattos, they had to experience the plight of the enslaved woman that entailed these cruel but common sexual violations. Jacobs, as Beardslee states in her "Through Slave Culture's Lens Comes Abundant Source: Harriet A. Jacobs's Incidents in the Life of a Salve Girl," "Cannot discuss her sexual past without expressing deep conflict" (37). In writing her narrative, Jacobs had to, in essence, relive these conflicts in great memory. These conflicts stem from the cruel behaviors of slave masters like Dr. Flint. Flint takes perversity to an extreme as he "[begins] to build a lonely cottage" (Jacobs 291) for the sole purpose of keeping his acts of sexual violations in secret from his own wife. Only female slaves experienced corruption to this extent. This is exactly why Harriet Jacobs, as Sekora states in his author biography, "Harriet Jacobs," "wished to write a book exposing the sexual exploitations of slave women." William Wells Brown's "Clotel; or, The President's Daughter" also vividly depicts accounts of sexual violations but from a different angle. Clotel was sold off in an auction block, but her sale price exponentially rose as the auctioneer exclaims, "The chastity of this girl is pure" (Brown 330). Divulging into the confines of the perverse, Clotel's virginity was being sold before her very eyes. This sexual violation of her purity and innocence was inevitable from the start of her life, her birth as a beautiful mulatto female.

As life was bestowed upon God, damnation simultaneously back tracked the lives of female mulattos. Linda Brent goes as far as describing that "slavery is terrible for men; but it is far more terrible for women" (Jacobs 294). Brent here expresses that male slaves did not have to pay the price of losing their virginity to the volitions of rape. As Jacobs and Brown have clearly exemplified, the female slave figure was less than the idea of being property of value in the hierarchal rank of the antebellum era. Granted, not all slave masters were vile and rotten to the extent of perverse indignity; however, it does not change the fact that these slaves were dehumanized. Jacobs and Brown's work both clearly pinpointed that by being a mulatto female slave, one must understand that "a raped slave was neither a person under criminal law nor property protected by civil law" (Stone 68). Jacobs and Brown's work sheds light on the irony and juxtaposition of the government at that time. Civil laws protect these citizens, but their involvement in slavery are by no means civil actions. Rather, they practice in torturous behaviors that pin the lives of many slaves. These behaviors taint the innocence and spirits of the youthful females as "the figure of the vulnerable girl is tied to the absent of figuration of woman as fully human" (Gilmore and Marshall 667). Seeing as how countless violations degraded the female identity, womanhood in all sense is shattered and destroyed. "Incidents in the Life of a Slave Girl" and "Clotel; or, The President's Daughter" similarly takes the convoluted and twisted idea of slavery and exploit its dark array of existence as both works take a cruel chapter in history and turn it into a lesson for future generations.

Dealing with constant grief and oppression, these two female mulattos took refuge in God. Not only was religion a prominent factor in the lives of both Linda Brent and Clotel, religion in general was a great catalyst of strength and determination in many slaves. The turmoil over life and death was a constant conflict in the life of a slave girl. When the institution of slavery burdened the soul and weaken the heart, the slaves looked to God for some sort of help and divine intervention. As seen in Jacobs's "Incidents in the Life of a Slave Girl," Linda Brent was touched by the grace of her savior after her success at running away from the south. This touch of grace restored Brent's hope, and faith "thrilled through [her] heart, and inspired [her] with trust in God" (Jacobs 305). The entire idea of a savior, a deliverer, gave Brent strong conviction in faith, reviving her much needed hope in the times of tragedies.

Translating religious comfort onto Brown's work, Clotel found refuge in God as well. She deliberately defied the slavery institution, and she ultimately took her own life to be with her savior. In the black culture the "deceased are considered just as much regarded …as the living" (Beardslee 55); therefore, rather slaves die and rid themselves from the evils of the world and still be regarded than be alive and in constant agony. Clotel shrouded her mind in the sanctuary of her religion, for "Christianity [needed] all her meekness to forgive [slavery]" (Brown 330). Jacobs and Brown proudly used the elements of religion in their work to show the readers that there was a higher divine power that allowed these slaves to survive as long as they did under the mayhem of slavery.

Adding concern to the mayhem of slavery, the perception of the white citizens, "are not necessarily to blame for the suffering of slaves, slavery is" (Schell 55). Jacobs and Brown's literary works vividly describe the slavery institution and fires all of their criticism and anger towards slavery itself, not primarily towards the whites that practiced it because to them this was the status quo. They never knew anything different— they saw no fault in the institution. "Incidents in the Life of a Slave Girl" and "Clotel; or, The President's Daughter" show that the manifestation and overall existence of slavery was a puppeteer, and the whites and slaves unfortunately had to be the puppets. Literary works hold of great importance to society for they enlighten the people of great history and lessons from each minutia of detail. Harriet Jacobs's "Incidents in the Life of a Slave Girl" and William Wells Brown's "Clotel; or, The President's Daughter" were no exception. These two iconic literary pieces shed light on what it was like to be a slave through the expense of two female mulatto slaves, Clotel and Linda Brent. These two slaves personified tragedy to its greatest extent as both suffered the pain from unfortunate events born from their identity as beautiful, innocent females.

Works Cited

Beardslee, Karen E. "Through Slave Culture's Lens Comes the Abundant Sources: Harriet A. Jacobs's Incident in the Life of a Slave Girl." *MELUS.* 1999. 22, 37. 200. *Literary Reference Center.* Web. 27 March 2011.

Brown, William W. "Clotel; or, The President's Daughter." *The Norton Anthology of African American Literature.* Ed. Henry Louis Gates, Jr. and Nellie Y. McKay. New York: W. W. Norton & Company, 2004. 325-345. Print.

Gilmore, Leigh and Elizabeth Marshall. "Girls in Crisis: Rescue and Transnational Feminist Autobiography Resistance." *Feminist Studies.* 36.3(2010): 667-690. *Literary Reference Center.* Web. 27 March 2011.

Jacobs, Harriet. "Incidents in the Life of a Slave Girl." *The Norton Anthology of African American Literature.* Ed. Henry Louis Gates, Jr. and Nellie Y. McKay. New York: W. W. Norton & Company, 2004. 280-315. Print.

Schell, Jenner. ""This Life is a Stage" : Performing the South in William Wells Brown's Clotel or, The President's Daughter." *University of Southern Mississippi.* 2008. 48-69. *Literary Reference Center.* Web. 27 March 2011.

Sekora, John. "Harriet Jacobs." *Salem Press.* 2003. 1-2. *Literary Reference Center.* Web. 27 March 2011.

Stone, Andrea. "Interracial Sexual Abuse and Legal Subjectivity in Antebellum Law and Literature." *American Literature.* 2009. 65-92. *Academic Search Complete.* Web. 27 March 2011.

***

Why I Like This Essay: Hendry's essay "How the Females Once Wept" is a wonderful illustration of the female mulatto slave. As with so many students, writing a research paper sometimes presents a few challenges. For Hendry, he was able to gather his thoughts and construct the essay using specific details and examples from the text and outside sources while maintaining the focus of the assignment. I sensed the pain of the slaves from the beginning to the end of his essay. Great job, Hendry.

Na Keya Bazemore, Instructor of English

Diamonds in the Rough

"I'm only 24, but I really want some piece."

"With so many different forms of entertainment, why would you want to live the city for anything."

"Peer pressure is what effects us the most."

"Their are no worries in the world."

"Professors in college accept you to be an target with all of your work."

"I was paid seven dollars and hour."

"If you have a well-rounded GPA, you could be offered to go out of state for collage."

"In the city, I do not need to worry about going to great distances to fine a grocery store."

"Some students do not try their best because they might not won't to seem like nerds."

"In the city, a good Samaritan is a thing of the passed."

"The earliest humans gather together in small communities."

Contributors

Joshua Brinson
Towers High School
Atlanta, Georgia

Julianna Casabonne
Lakeside High School
Atlanta, Georgia

Quan Chen
Duluth High School
Duluth, Georgia

Gabriel Diaz
Faith Academy
Stockbridge, Georgia

De'Lamoore Downie
Immaculate Conception HS
Jamaica

Jasmine Eccles
Stone Mountain HS
Stone Mountain, Georgia

Nathan Ellison
Milton High School
Alpharetta, Georgia

Dericka Gale
John F. Kennedy HS
Cleveland, Ohio

Kelly Hill Hall
Milton High School
Alpharetta, Georgia

Taneka Hightower
Thomas Jefferson HS
Rockford, Illinois

Jessica Joiner
Atlanta, Georgia

Alberta Jones
Durham High School
Durham, North Carolina

Tuan Minh Khong
Clarkston High School
Clarkston, Georgia

Walker Kirkland
Christa McAuliffe Academy
Yahima, Washington

Hendry Kurniawan
Berkmar High School
Lilburn, Georgia

Yaroslav Kuznyetsov
Lakeside High School
Atlanta, Georgia

Sompong Liwwayha

Melanie McElroy

Genevieve D. Milliken
Mount Carmel Academy
New Orleans, Louisana

Bryce Monaco
Camas High School
Camas, Washington

Doriyana Monconduit

Elizabeth Morris
Roswell High School
Roswell, Georgia

Philip Nethers
Westview High School
Portland, Oregon

Calvin Oliver
Benjamin E. Mays HS
Atlanta, Georgia

David Payne
Goose Creek High School
Goose Creek, SC

Crystal Shahid
Mohammed Schools of Atl.
Atlanta, Georgia

Demetrius Sharp
Atlanta, Georgia

Cindy Sok
Centennial High School
Roswell, Georgia
Jeremy Stipcak

Berkmar High School
Lawrenceville, Georgia

Robel Teklehuimunot
Clarkston High School
Clarkston, Georgia

Chiemeka R. Ugochukwu
King's College Lagos
Lagos, Nigeria

Alexandra Van de Water
Independence High School
Roswell, Georgia

Edward Wanambwa

Abebaw Woldehana
Arbaminch High School
Arbaminch, Ethiopia